Las Vegas

Berlitz®
Las Vegas

Text by James P. Reza with contributions by
  Matthew R. Poole
Photography: Matthew R. Poole, Las Vegas
Convention Authority, Las Vegas News Bureau,
Doug Traverso, pp. 72, 85 ©Caesar's Palace, p.
34 © Bellagio Hotel, p. 83 © Al Seib, p. 69 ©
Doug Plummer 1998
Cover photograph by Matthew R. Poole
Photo Editor: Naomi Zinn
Layout: Media Content Marketing, Inc.
Cartography by Ortelius Design
Managing Editor: Tony Halliday

Tenth Edition 2002

CONTACTING THE EDITORS
Every effort has been made to provide accurate information in this publication, but
changes are inevitable. The publisher cannot be responsible for any resulting loss,
inconvenience or injury. We would appreciate it if readers would call our attention to
any errors or outdated information by contacting Berlitz Publishing, PO Box 7910,
London SE1 1WE, England. Fax: (44) 20 7403 0290;
e-mail: berlitz@apaguide.demon.co.uk

CONTENTS

• A (☞) in the text denotes a highly recommended sight

Las Vegas

LAS VEGAS
AND ITS PEOPLE

It is hard to believe that Las Vegas—a city of mythic pro-
portion—started out as little more than a dusty railroad
stop in the middle of a barren and unforgiving desert valley.
It is harder still to understand the dramatic changes that
would occur in the valley over the course of the 20th century,
which created the city known today as the "Entertainment
Capital of the World."

Though initially settled in the mid 1800s, Las Vegas struggled as a Mormon outpost for much of its early existence. It
was not recognized as an official town until 1905. On 15
May of that year, railroad officials from the San Pedro, Los
Angeles, and Salt Lake Railroad stood at the intersection of
Main and Fremont streets (where the Plaza Hotel now
stands) and auctioned 1200 lots of railroad land mapped
from 40 square blocks of desert dust. Within a year, the city's
population had grown to 1500 brave pioneers, though the
only visitors were train passengers on their way to a real city.

Nine decades later, today's cascade of visitors is surrounded by the fastest growing, most rapidly changing
metropolis the American West has ever known. They stroll
wide-eyed in the shadows of the landmarks of the world's
greatest cities; around them, within walking distance of one
another, loom replicas of the Eiffel Tower, a massive pyramid of Egypt, and the palaces of ancient Rome.

In a testament to Las Vegas's relentless pursuit of illusion,
its modern visitors never recognize the landmarks that originally offered the city its shot at history: its natural springs,
most of which have long since run empty. Though water
flows freely through the city's multitude of artificial lakes,

lush resort swimming areas, and sprinklers quenching the famous golf courses, it now arrives via a giant pipeline connected to the Colorado River. Without that pipeline, the city would most certainly dry up and crumble back into the desert.

Notable as the only major American city built in the twentieth century, Las Vegas is particularly unfettered by any burden of history or preservation. As old—some would say historically significant—buildings or resorts succumb to the pressures of age, design, or simple decline of attendance (and therefore value), the law of the city takes over. The buildings are completely remodeled, or, at the extreme, reinvented as the sites of grand implosions accompanied by fireworks, parties, and general street-wide celebration. Few will remember, or perhaps even care, that the Italian-themed Venetian (complete with Colorado-fed canals) is built upon the site of the Rat Pack's most famous haunt, the Sands Hotel-Casino. Today, Italy; tomorrow, who knows?

Las Vegas, like every good gambler, has worked hard to reinvent and renegotiate its future. After more than a decade of conversion from an insider Mob town to a family-friendly attraction for Middle America, Las Vegas is again on the verge of its next phase—top notch resort city. Today's Las Vegas reigns as one of the world's most popular travel and vacation destinations. World class accommodations, five-star dining, and shopping opportunities that rival every major city have added immeasurably to the city's reputation for all-night gambling, drinking, and adult-oriented temptations. Hotel-casinos have repositioned themselves as complete resorts, offering full-service day spas, huge shopping malls, and attraction-filled theme parks—all in addition to the gambling, golf courses, and showrooms of the past.

New resorts, such as the Bellagio, are aimed at travelers attempting to recapture the glamour of the Rat Pack era, while many others are following the lead of Caesars Palace, which offers world-class shopping facilities. This trend toward building complete resorts is perhaps the best approach attempted in recent years, since it offers something for everyone. Always betting on the side of growth, expansion, and the power of positive cash flow, Las Vegas has again transformed itself and emerged as much more than a water stop for thirsty pioneers.

Such rapid change and reinvention results in what many call a city without a soul. But for its over one million residents and 30 million annual visitors, it is this very characteristic—namely

Las Vegas, the realm of the fabulous and the fantastic, welcomes you 24 hours a day.

the city's uncanny ability to sense the next big thing, or failing that, to create one—that makes Las Vegas the city of their dreams. In fact, many of the 30 million annual visitors choose to stay. For nearly a decade, new residents have numbered almost four thousand per month, pushing the recent population of the valley up near 1.3 million—a nearly 1000 percent increase since that fateful railroad auction of 1905.

Outside the resort corridors, new suburban residential developments have swallowed the surrounding desert, eagerly edging to the bases of the easterly and westerly mountain

With idyllic scenes like this not far from the Strip, it's easy to see where Las Vegas, or "the meadows," got its name.

ranges. Unlike the original American suburbs, new master-planned communities like Summerlin and Green Valley are cities within themselves; in fact, they boast more square miles and more amenities than Las Vegas itself. New businesses spring up almost immediately, built into the plan and ready to serve an already-waiting group of customers. Driving through these areas feels like traversing a movie set—the homes sparkling and new, the roadways smooth and wide, the landscaping young and fragile.

There are those who leave the city as well. For the four thousand a month who come to stay, approximately two thousand others pack up their belongings and head elsewhere, still searching for what brought them to Las Vegas in the first place. The American Dream is alive and well here, but it has little patience for losers. This is part of the unrelenting psyche of the place. Although the motto of Las Vegas is that everyone is a winner, for the most part, it is a city unforgiving of failure.

Still, despite all this rapid growth, incessant change, and unsettling population turnover, there certainly is a core city, and there certainly are long-time residents, many who proudly call themselves natives.

Driving in the central city, within a few miles of Downtown, one passes the neighborhoods of Charleston Heights and the Huntridge, where plaster-walled and wood-floored houses reign, often still occupied by the original residents. Not far from these modest areas are the city's first upscale developments, Rancho Circle and the Scotch 80s. Here, just a short mile or so from Fremont Street and Glitter Gulch, are quiet, ranch-style homes spread out over parcels of an acre (about ½ hectare) or more, complete with swimming pools, tennis courts, horse corrals, and lush, mature landscaping. These neighborhoods, often overlooked as "too Downtown" by newcomers, are what longer established cities would consider treasures.

It is here, in neighborhoods like these, that a sense of the need for continuity and community is emerging. In many core neighborhoods of all income classes, voices are being raised about the necessity of neighborhood preservation, about community service, and about offering broad-based opportunities and experiences for children growing up in "Sin City."

These concerns are not really new to Las Vegas; they had simply been overshadowed by growth in recent years. Today, many long-time residents as well as newcomers are seeking to regain a sense of security in the rapidly changing landscape, a city in which one could leave the doors unlocked at night just thirty years ago. Through civic organizations and neighborhood preservation groups, they are working hard toward a renewal of that sense of community lost in the hustle.

Also beyond the Strip and Downtown lie other signs of a real living and breathing metropolis. The University of Nevada-Las Vegas boasts a student population over 23,000 (though, like most of the people in Las Vegas, they are commuters). Before its recent rapid expansion, the city claimed to have more churches per capita than any other in the United States. (Apparently spiritual guidance was a necessity for those who dwelt among an excess of temptation.)

And though today's Las Vegas is still dominated by the gambling industry, non-gaming business has flourished here as well, thanks to the county's and state's favorable tax structure. Much of the non-gaming business resides in suburban business parks and master-planned communities, part of the city's effort to reinvent the nature of urban and suburban existence by offering multiple industrial and retail centers throughout the valley. Credit card companies and banks, mail order firms, health care subsidiaries, and high-tech software developers all contribute to a healthy local economy, helping to diversify Las Vegas in the face of an ever-changing national gambling landscape.

Moreover, Las Vegas has recently started to show signs of maturity in its cultural status as well. Long dismissed as a gaudy playground of excess, Las Vegas has seen recent spurts of cultural growth. Local theater is healthy, a first-class public art museum recently opened, and there are encouraging signs that a centrally located arts and retail district known as The Gateway will soon erupt from its upstart beginnings into a major draw for residents and tourists alike.

Likewise, Las Vegas remains one of the few cities in the nation with two competing daily newspapers. There are also dozens of smaller newspapers serving a variety of specific interests, including two dueling alternative weeklies.

***One of the new pleasure palaces in town, the Bellagio is a
luxe ideal of the trend toward resort-style accommodations.***

As Las Vegas embarks on the new millennium, one can
sense an attempt by the city to accept its disparities, to come
to grips with the nature of its own existence and place in
America, and to thoughtfully wrestle with the challenges of
its future. While it confronts the issues that all growing cities
face—crime, growth, challenges to its industry—Las Vegas
seems to know that it has within its grasp the chance to rank
among the world's great cities, to show what America's only
20th-century metropolis can accomplish.

Las Vegas's transformation from a lowly watering hole to
a gambling and prostitution stop, to a desert retreat for Hollywood heavyweights, and finally to an international resort city
is part of an eternal metamorphosis. A city living with one
eye open to the future prevents life here from ever being boring, and also attracts tourists by the millions to experience the
Las Vegas life, if only for a few glittering moments.

A BRIEF HISTORY

Early Habitation

The inhabited history of the Las Vegas Valley stretches to 23,000 B.C., when much of the area was covered by a prehistoric lake. During this period, the indigenous people lived in caves, hunting the mammals that gathered at the shoreline. The landscape of the valley changed dramatically over the next 200 centuries. The glaciers feeding the lake melted away and the lake evaporated. Fossils tell an obscure story of man's slow and sporadic development.

Around 3000 B.C., native Archaic Indians began to develop a lasting hunting and gathering culture. By this time, the valley was in much the same geographic state as it exists in today, with one exception—the presence of artesian springs that bubbled to the surface in several areas. These springs fed a network of streams draining through the Las Vegas Wash to the Colorado River. The areas surrounding the springs were desert oases: sprawling collections of grasses, trees, and wildlife. Many springs lay in areas that would eventually become the center of the modern Las Vegas metropolis.

For about 4000 years, the Archaics thrived in a culture that included many signs of early civilization. Signs of even more advancement appeared halfway through the first millennium A.D., when the Anasazi Indians inhabited the valley. Far more progressive than the Archaics, the Anasazi utilized such formal agricultural techniques as irrigation to assist their harvest. This permitted the Anasazi to achieve a benchmark of advanced society—the ability to live in permanent shelters year-round without need to follow wildlife. Mysteriously, the Anasazi vanished from the valley around A.D. 1150, leaving it to be repopulated by the Southern Paiutes, another hunter-gatherer tribe.

*The red sandstone at Valley of Fire State Park still shows
traces of the earliest Las Vegas inhabitants.*

Unable to replicate the agricultural techniques of the
Anasazi, the Paiutes were destined to a semi-nomadic
lifestyle until European settlers arrived, changing the nature
of existence in the valley forever.

From Mailmen to Mormons

In the early nineteenth century, America's western territories
were still largely unexplored. It was not until 1829 that Rafael
Rivera, a Mexican scout, found a spring-fed valley and dubbed
it *Las Vegas*—a Spanish name that leaves many modern visitors wondering exactly where "the meadows" really lay.

For fifteen years, Las Vegas was used as a Spanish Trail
way-station. In 1844, American explorer John C. Fremont
parked his horses at Big Springs, and his report to the government resulted in a mail route leading past the spot on its

Las Vegas's destiny was ordained by the rail connection made in 1905 between Los Angeles and Salt Lake City.

way to California. This put Las Vegas on the map and was one of the crucial turning points of its history.

In 1855, Mormon leader Brigham Young responded to promising reports of Las Vegas by sending 30 missionary settlers to the valley; they eventually built a fort not far from today's Downtown. Surrounded by acres of farmland hewn from the hard desert, the adobe fort became a focal point for the development of Las Vegas for the next fifty years. The missionaries struggled valiantly against the dictates of the desert, trying simultaneously to survive the harshness of their circumstances and spread the Mormon faith. Additional pressures from arriving miners pushed the missionaries' plight beyond recovery. Their supplies scarce, their harvest meager, and their spirit broken, they abandoned the fort in 1858.

Despite the fact that the local land was rich in silver, by 1865 most of the mining traffic through Las Vegas was of prospectors headed to California or Northern Nevada in search of gold. One opportunist who stayed was Octavius Decatur Gass. Bestowed with plenty of the invaluable pioneer spirit that characterizes Las Vegas to this day, Gass redirected his life by picking up where the Mormons left off—at least when it came to ranching and farming. Gass took over the abandoned Mormon fort and 640 acres (260 hectares) surrounding it, dubbing it the Las Vegas Ranch. He expanded the ranch and irrigated the land so that it would support crops and cattle. His determination had other results as well: Gass was named a justice of the peace and a territorial legislator.

Despite his ambition, Gass' success was short-lived. In the late 1870s, he defaulted on a loan from rancher Archibald Stewart, so Stewart took the Las Vegas Ranch for his own. True to wild-West stereotypes, Stewart was slain by a neighboring farmer, leaving his strong-willed wife, Helen, to assume the duties of the ranch. Through 1905, Helen Stewart expanded the ranch to 2000 acres (810 hectares), making quite a bit of money in the process.

What happened next would mark the end of the successful Las Vegas Ranch and the beginning of the era of the subdivision seen across almost all of Western America to this day. The railroad was coming, and when it arrived, Las Vegas would never be the same again.

Of Tracks and Tracts

At the turn of the 19th century Los Angeles and Salt Lake City were among the burgeoning metropolises of the new American West. Though the two cities remained unlinked by rail, this was about to change quickly. When it did, the Las

Vegas Valley (which at the time had a non-native population of less than 30) would change as well.

In 1903, officials of the San Pedro, Los Angeles, and Salt Lake Railroad arrived in Las Vegas, eager to secure a right-of-way for their Los Angeles–Salt Lake connection. Las Vegas would serve as a major stopover for crew rest and train repair. For all this, the railroad needed land. As mapped, the track traveled directly through Helen Stewart's Las Vegas Ranch. Stewart sold 99.5 percent of her ranch to the railroad. The remainder she returned to the native Paiutes.

In early 1905, the route between Los Angeles and Salt Lake City was completed, and train tracks bore right down the center of the Las Vegas Valley. On 15 May 1905, the railroad held a land sale—a momentous step in Las Vegas history. Standing at the depot at Main and Fremont streets, railroad officials auctioned 1200 lots they had subdivided from forty square blocks of desert scrub. Land speculators and locals alike were anxious to own a part of the newest railroad boomtown, and within an afternoon, more than 80 percent of the lots were sold.

> Las Vegas is the only city in America where the phone book is published twice a year.

Las Vegas was no longer a small pioneer settlement. With rail service in place and forty blocks of private property, it was ready to become a real town. Businesses sprang up overnight, and wooden houses were erected to replace the tent city in which many of the early settlers had lived. One year after the auction, the population of Las Vegas had ballooned to 1500 residents, a portent of things to come for the next ninety years.

Dam Good Luck

From the beginning, Las Vegas was built to serve travelers. The railroad needed a way station, and Las Vegas was the place. Growth continued for ten years, and by 1915 the town had telephones, round-the-clock electricity, and a growing population—many of whom worked in the railroad repair shop. But such heady progress would soon come to a halt.

The growing competition in rail transport resulted in Union Pacific buying the Los Angeles–Salt Lake line. Union Pacific then consolidated its operations, eliminating the Las Vegas repair facility. Additionally, Las Vegas had been made a part of Nevada's new Clark County in 1909, a year when the legislature also outlawed

Hoover Dam brought in thousands of new residents and the water they required.

gambling. These unfortunate circumstances threatened to relegate Las Vegas to the status of a small desert community that could no longer support its 3000 residents. But the southwest's growing need for water, combined with Las Vegas's fortuitous proximity to the Colorado River, would give Las Vegas a second chance to achieve prosperity.

Construction on Hoover Dam (originally Boulder Dam, subsequently renamed for the president who authorized the project) began in 1931 in a canyon 45 miles (72 km) southeast of Las Vegas. Providing an influx of $165 million to the southwestern economy, Hoover Dam played a major role in preventing Las Vegas from drying up, both financially and literally. Not only did it create jobs, but it also created Lake Mead, the massive reservoir that today provides water to all of southern Nevada.

More Government Help

The construction of Hoover Dam did not single-handedly save Las Vegas, however. The state legislature helped as well, by legalizing gambling in 1931 and thus solidifying the future of the town, though legislators and residents could never have known this at the time.

The hordes of people who attended Hoover Dam's 1935 dedication set the city's now-formidable public relations machine into action. They went to work on what has become one of the lengthiest citywide tourism campaigns ever

The Sahara Hotel and Casino is one of the most historic establishments on the Strip.

attempted. It didn't take long for the city to establish itself as a wild-West town with an "anything goes" attitude. Vices outlawed or heavily controlled elsewhere were legal here, available any hour of any day (or night). Thus originated Las Vegas's reputation as an adult theme park.

Additional catalysts for the valley's growth came from World War II. Both the Las Vegas Aerial Gunnery School (which became Nellis Air Force Base and the Nevada Test Site) in the north, and Basic Magnesium in the nearby town of Henderson, arrived in the early 1940s as a result of America's war effort. By 1945, the population had grown to almost 20,000, with workers and airmen moving in at a rapid pace. But this was not yet the Las Vegas of folklore.

Mobsters and Rat Packers

While many gambling halls opened Downtown in the 1930s and early 1940s, only two were built on the stretch of old Los Angeles Highway that ultimately became the Strip. The El Rancho Vegas (1941) was the first, followed by the Last Frontier (1943). During this period, East Coast Syndicate member Benjamin "Bugsy" Siegel earned a foothold as a local casino operator.

> **Las Vegas is Spanish for "the meadows."**

By 1945 Siegel had become one of Las Vegas's original visionaries, planning an opulent resort on the southern end of the LA Highway. When the Flamingo opened in December 1946, it did so with Hollywood flair and the new Vegas flash. But the Mafia bosses who financed the operation were displeased with its performance; Siegel was murdered in the summer of 1947.

Despite its initial failings, Siegel's Flamingo survived him, as did mob infiltration of casinos. In fact, the Flamingo would launch over two decades of strong mob presence in Las Vegas. Freely flowing "comps" (complimentary food, drink, and entertainment) were the order of the day, with mob bosses content to provide an environment of pleasurable excess as long as the cash kept rolling in.

While the mob was running the casinos, promoters were busily selling Las Vegas as a glamorous Hollywood in the desert. From the mid-1940s to the mid-1960s, Las Vegas nurtured a growing sense that it was the "Entertainment Capital of the World." Emerging stars, no longer content with playing small nightclubs, came to Las Vegas with dreams of making it big. Many of them did. Frank Sinatra, Wayne Newton, and Louis Prima each arrived with mediocre status and suddenly found themselves with names as big as the marquees on which they were written. The Rat Pack—originally Frank Sinatra, Dean Martin, Sammy Davis Jr., Peter Lawford, and Joey Bishop, all in town to film *Ocean's 11*—landed at the Sands in January 1960 for a legendary stay. Other Hollywood stars came as well, simply because Las Vegas was the place to be.

As a result, more casinos emerged along the Strip. The Thunderbird, Desert Inn, Sahara, Sands, and Riviera hotels were erected during this period, luring a curious clientele drawn by tales of all-night partying, exclusive entertainment, and cheap accommodations. There was no longer any question: when you wanted some unbridled adult fun, Las Vegas was the place to be.

New Legitimacy

Organized crime was soon to have a formidable adversary in its bid to control Las Vegas—corporate cash. Though Las Vegas had developed a powerful local economy, few major outside investments were made in the city, due primarily to mob infiltration and its inherent ties to illegal activities.

That would change dramatically with the 1966 arrival of billionaire Howard Hughes. A legitimate businessman,

Hughes was nonetheless eccentric and dramatic, a style suited to the Las Vegas ethos. True to the myth, the reclusive Hughes immediately cloistered himself in the Desert Inn's penthouse. Several weeks later he was asked—then ordered—to vacate the room to make room for high rollers, whereupon he promptly bought the property and fired the management. Thus began Hughes' legendary three-year, $300-million Las Vegas buying spree. When it was over, Hughes owned six casinos, an airport, and an airline, along with numerous plots of land stretching from the Strip to the mountains.

Hughes' actions would have beneficial repercussions, both immediate and lasting. Because of the new legitimacy Las Vegas acquired from Hughes' investments, established companies such as Hilton Hotels bought into the gaming business, and their influence helped draw a line in the desert sand between legitimate operations and mob casinos, where illegal skimming of profits was rampant. That, combined with the formation of the Nevada Gaming Control Board, would signal the beginning of the end for heavy mob influence in the city.

Las Vegas with a Vision

As corporations moved in and the mob was slowly pushed out, a new Las Vegas emerged. The legitimization of gambling led to its increased legalization across the US. What was once a sure thing became much more competitive. Casino operators had to reassess the nature of their business.

The first to really do so was Steve Wynn, a Las Vegas resident and owner of the Golden Nugget. In the mid-1980s, Wynn began plans to reinvigorate Las Vegas with a new resort. He bought several Strip properties—the Silver Slipper and Castaways among them—and demolished them to make way for a new kind of resort—Mirage—which became an instant success.

Wynn's demolition of the existing properties started a trend that, more than any other, describes Las Vegas at the end of the 20th century: removal of old properties in exchange for the potential of new ones. This trend has led to many more demolitions, including the Dunes (replaced by Bellagio), Aladdin (the new Aladdin) and Sands (Venetian) hotels.

Wynn's casinos have also set new standards. They can no longer be just a box filled with gaming tables, restaurants, and a showroom. Excalibur, the MGM Grand, the Luxor, and New York-New York all followed Mirage's lead during the 1990s, offering themed environments and attractions for families.

As evidence of the "ever-faster" nature of the city, by the middle of the 1990s the new approach showed signs of backlash, with many visitors criticizing the mediocrity of the Las Vegas experience. The latest approach is perhaps the best of the post-mob era: the comprehensive resort. New resorts offer attractions and amenities modeled after those available in top resort cities worldwide, including luxurious spas, signature restaurants, and exclusive boutiques.

Additionally, a handful of resorts—such as the South-Seas themed Mandalay Bay, the Mirage, and the Four Seasons—are now catering exclusively to the luxury travel market. The crème de la crème of Las Vegas deluxe is Steve Wynn's Bellagio. The world's most expensive resort at $1.6 billion, the Bellagio's amenities include 5-star dining, Chanel-caliber boutiques, and a world-class collection of artistic masterworks. Perhaps more important, such high-end accommodations raise the standards of expectations back to the mythology of the Rat Pack era.

As it changed from mob gambling town to corporate gaming venue, the population of Las Vegas skyrocketed. Over 20,000 additional hotel rooms have been added in a few short years, including resorts in Summerlin and Lake Las Vegas.

New York in Las Vegas: hotel themes just keep getting more and more spectacular.

Recent business projections for Las Vegas predict challenges; tourism revenues must increase substantially to sustain what is already built, while actual figures show visitation as steady or declining. The growth that has characterized Las Vegas for nearly a century may be facing a roadblock.

Still, the future of Las Vegas is sure to be determined as much by the pioneering spirit that built the city as by anything else. With its new look and new aim, the prospects are good despite the warnings. Inevitably, some people will get burned in the process, but others will rise triumphantly from the fray to even greater successes. And that, more than anything, is the one constant that characterizes the past, present, and future of Las Vegas.

WHERE TO GO

THE STRIP

Since Bugsy Siegel's Flamingo set a new standard in 1946, nothing in the world rivals the Strip's audacity or the casinos' desire to outdo each other. This 3½ mile (5½ km) section of the old Los Angeles Highway is notorious the world over for its blatant, unending decadence. Stretching from the new Mandalay Bay resort in the south to the Stratosphere tower further north, this portion of Las Vegas Boulevard South has evoked more melodrama and mythology than the rest of the city and its history combined.

Miles of neon tubing and millions of dazzling incandescent and fiber optic lights illuminate every hour of darkness year round, while casinos that never close leave the doors to their comfortably air-conditioned interiors wide open, even while the summer sun burns down at 115° F (46° C). It's hard to overlook such devilish excess, but the visitors don't come to ignore; rather, they come to indulge.

An armada of resorts, shops, restaurants, and—of course—glittering casinos line both sides of the thoroughfare, tantalizing onlookers. Dozens of the world's largest hotels are situated directly in the action, simply because the hotels *are* the major attractions. Some of these mega-resorts cling to the cliches of the past, while others attempt a chic that borders on the unreal. Roman palaces, the Eiffel Tower, the pyramids of Egypt, and the jungles of Polynesia all await anyone who wishes to indulge in extravagance and can afford the trip.

At the southern-most end of the Strip, the **Mandalay Bay Resort and Casino**, 3950 Las Vegas Boulevard South, is one of its newest resorts. The $950-million behemoth features 3700 rooms, including a unique "hotel-within-a-hotel":

Could it be said any clearer? Games of chance, risk, skill, and luck will always be the top attraction in Las Vegas.

424 rooms managed by the renowned Four Seasons (see below). Central to the jungle-city theme is an 11-acre (4½-hectare) tropical environment complete with a wave pool that beats upon a sandy beach. Also included: a House of Blues restaurant and club, a 1700-seat showroom (staging "Chicago"), a 12,000-seat arena, and a 30,000-sq-ft (2790-sq-m) spa. Some restaurants include Charlie Palmer's Aureole, China Grill, Wolfgang Puck's Trattoria del Lupo, and the trendy vodka bar Red Square.

The Four Seasons company, renowned for its superlative attention to guests' needs (poor customer service is a major complaint at most Las Vegas resorts), has created one of Las Vegas's only non-gaming resorts within the Mandalay Bay, the

The Luxor Hotel and Casino is home to the world's largest atrium and some relatively convincing Egyptian "artifacts."

Four Seasons Hotel Las Vegas. A total of 424 ultra-luxury accommodations occupy floors 35 to 39 of the Mandalay Bay tower, reachable only via a private, Four Seasons lobby elevator. A separate driveway leads to a two-story main building housing the lobby, four restaurants and bars, health spa, and meeting rooms. An 8000-sq-ft (744-sq-m) pool set in a lush garden is available only to Four Seasons guests. If your priorities are comfort first and gambling second, this hotel is for you.

Forget the wimpy Egyptian pyramids—the mighty black monolith of the **Luxor Hotel and Casino**, 3900 Las Vegas Boulevard South, is 30 stories of tinted glass and steel topped with a night-defiant laser that screams, "Come on in, we're open!" Encompassing the world's largest atrium, the pyramid (and its two adjoining towers) house over 4000 rooms and a stunningly huge but dull casino decorated with faux Egyptian artifacts. There are attractions worth noting, though, including the Oasis Spa, Ra nightclub, 3-D IMAX movie theater, 12 restaurants, a motion-simulator ride, and a two-story **Sega Virtual Land**—a prototype of video arcades of the future. Perhaps the biggest thrill is getting to your room, which involves a ride on the "inclinator," an elevator that moves up and sideways at the same time. For a silly souvenir, have your photo taken next to the ten-story Sphinx that guards the front entrance.

The smallest and oldest of the four resorts at the busy intersection of Las Vegas Boulevard and Tropicana Avenue, the **Tropicana Resort and Casino**, 3801 Las Vegas Boulevard South, ignored the family-aimed marketing of the 1990s and held rather tightly to the notion of Las Vegas as an adult escape. The main showroom's "Folies Bergères" has wooed audiences with its topless showgirls since 1961. The understated class of the hotel tower may have lost some luster but still retains an air of respectability, while the tropical pool area (with swim-up blackjack tables) remains nearly perfect.

The first themed property to follow the Mirage, the **Excalibur Hotel and Casino**, 3850 Las Vegas Boulevard South, is a Renaissance Faire aimed squarely at families or travelers on a budget. This is evident in the execution—though not at all shoddy, the overall experience is comparatively average. For a brief period the Excalibur was the largest hotel in the world at 4008 rooms, surpassed later by the MGM Grand. Its most interesting aspect is the showroom's "King Arthur's Tournament," a live re-creation of a Middle Ages jousting tournament and one of the few dinner shows left in Las Vegas. The 100,000-sq-ft (9300-sq-m) casino, which caters mostly to minimum betters, has plenty of $3 blackjack tables and nickel and dime slot machines. The resort, like most of Las Vegas, looks best at night—the brightly illuminated spires are quite majestic when viewed from the Strip.

Taking the art of theming to its extreme, the **New York-New York Hotel and Casino**, 3790 Las Vegas Boulevard South, actually spawned lawsuits by Manhattan architects. Its dozen towers are uncanny, one-third-size replicas of famous New York skyscrapers, including the Empire State building, New York Public Library, and Chrysler building. Inside, the detailed illusion continues with near-Disney quality, such as the fake subway station (complete with graffiti), Coney Island arcade, and 84,000-sq-ft (7812-sq-m) casino area fashioned after Central Park—right down to the tress, footbridges, and street lamps. The Greenwich Village dining environment nearly overshadows the food, but the Motown Cafe can do wonders for your musical palate. The Empire Bar is a classy after-hours spot, and the **Manhattan Express** roller coaster is worth the long wait.

One of the world's largest hotels, the **MGM Grand Hotel and Casino**, 3799 Las Vegas Boulevard South, is so massive—the casino floor alone is the size of four American football fields—that most visitors become completely disoriented as they wander the resort. Past guests may remember the overly cute Wizard of Oz theme, which has since been replaced

Play a good hand or eat with your hands: both are possible at the Renaissance- themed Excalibur.

(with a multi-million-dollar renovation) by a new, more mature theme that incorporates all of MGM's most famous movies. How big is big? Try 5034 guest rooms spread across 114 acres (46 hectares), 12 restaurants (including establishments by Wolfgang Puck, Emeril Lagasse, and Mark Miller), an elaborate 6½-acre (3-hectare) pool complex, a spa and tennis facility, three arenas, a comedy club, and the Studio 54 nightclub. There are four gaming areas, each with a different theme and minimum bets ranging from $5 to $500, as well as nearly four thousand slot machines and lively sports betting. The adjoining 18-acre (7-hectare)

MGM's establishment recalls the glitter of Hollywood and great films from the past.

theme park is mediocre at best, with one exception, the terrifying SkyScreamer. High rollers might be "lucky" enough to stay in one of 30 private villas at The Mansion.

The **Monte Carlo Hotel and Casino**, 3770 Las Vegas Boulevard South, evokes a classic Las Vegas atmosphere remarkably accessible to any traveler. Striking in its beautifully understated European theme, this resort captures an air of elegance hard to experience in modern Las Vegas. In homage to tradition, the resort offers a wide range of gaming, dining, retail, and spa amenities without a rush to create a family-friendly environment (though children are welcome in permitted areas). Though it looks like a haven for high rollers, minimum bets are actually quite modest, starting at $5; they even have 5-cent slots. The Lance Burton Theatre, a showcase for Lance Burton's highly entertaining and amusing magic act, is arguably the most magnificent showroom in the city.

Those who insist on the familiarity of a hotel chain will like the **Holiday Inn Boardwalk**, 3750 Las Vegas Boulevard South. Expect higher rates than the chain's usual; after all, this is prime real estate. Despite the façade of Coney Island-like attractions, the theming is not extensive. Disappointingly, none of the rides (including a carousel and roller coaster) are real.

Across the street, is the new **Aladdin Hotel and Casino**, 3667 Las Vegas Boulevard South. Out with the

The Monte Carlo passes on flash, instead opting for understated, accessible elegance.

1960s Aladdin (where Elvis Presley was married) and in with the 21st century version. Consisting of a unique property (with an adjoining property that will eventually become the Aladdin Music Project), the new Aladdin Hotel and Casino continues the long-running theme of Middle Eastern fantasy and legend. The hotel offers 2600 rooms, 150,000 sq ft (13,950 sq m) of gaming, and seven restaurants. There is also a showroom, performing arts theater, and the Desert Passage shopping promenade, which has an additional 14 restaurants..

Opened in 1999 is the **Paris Hotel and Casino**, 3655 Las Vegas Boulevard South. The theme scheme marches on with this massive $750-million, 2900-room hotel-casino, modeled after the Hotel de Ville in Paris. The rest of the property is caricature of its namesake city, complete with River Seine and Arc de Triomphe. Patrons can see the city lights from the top of the one-half scale Eiffel Tower, shop the Rue de la Paix, or dine in eight Parisian-inspired restaurants, including one in the Tower. Cobblestone walkways lead throughout the casino to other landmark replicas, including the Paris Opera House and the Louvre. Expect high minimum bets and more than 2,000 slot machines within the gilded casino.

One of the old guard of Las Vegas resorts, **Bally's Hotel and Casino**, 3645 Las Vegas Boulevard South, has suffered few transformations over the years. Despite the futuristic light-and-water show out front (a curious use of $14 million), Bally's is an exercise in classic Las Vegas style. Inside, it is comfortable and inviting, with dark colors and grand chandeliers hanging above the casino floor. Since Bally is the leading maker of gaming machines, you'll find all the latest video versions of poker, blackjack, craps, and roulette (a great place to learn how to play). The showroom features the adults-only "Jubilee!," while head-liners have included everyone from Penn and Teller to Paul Anka. Try the pricey but luxurious Sterling Brunch. Behind the casino is a monorail that offers free rides to MGM Grand.

The most lavish resort in Las Vegas is the 3000-room **Bellagio Hotel and Casino**, 3600 Las Vegas Boulevard South, a stunning replica of an Italian villa that boasts an equally stunning price tag: $1.6 billion dollars. Gaming rooms offer an unlikely quiet elegance, while the Gallery of Fine Art holds treasures bought from the world's finest collections. The dining is unparalleled, as are the luxurious accommodations. The 13,000-sq ft (1208-sq m) conservatory features a dazzling display of fauna. Also worth a look is the spectacularly chore-ographed water show in the small lake fronting the resort, as well as Cirque du Soleil's equally spectacular aquatic show called "O" (though tickets don't come cheap). One caveat:

shopping is reserved for big spenders, but it sure is fun to browse among the diamonds and furs.

A standard-setter since its 1968 opening, **Caesars Palace Hotel and Casino**, 3570 Las Vegas Boulevard South, is one of the few old-timers to keep pace with modern Las Vegas, perhaps because its ancient Rome theme was popular from the outset (that, and real marble never seems to go out of style). Here, elegance seems within reach of anyone, though having lots of money certainly helps. The casino is a high-roller's haven with lofty limits at many tables. Sports fans will enjoy the lively environment at the sports book. A new 29-story Palace Tower has raised the total number of rooms to almost 2,500. Additional new pleasantries include a fitness center and spa. The renowned **Forum Shops** offer a cornucopia of shops and restaurants catering to any budget. The Omnimax Theatre and IMAX 3-D motion simulator ride, both located in the Forum Shops, are also very popular.

The Bellagio's lovely Picasso Restaurant (left) and its Gallery of Fine Art (below).

35

Tiny by Strip standards, and occupying a powerful corner of the famed boulevard, the 200-room **Barbary Coast**, 3595 Las Vegas Boulevard South, begs the question: "How and why has it survived?" The rooms offer a charming and comfortable rendition of 1900 San Francisco, but the real draw of the hotel-casino is the recently added restaurant, Drai's. Already recognized as one of Las Vegas's best, Drai's arrived when Hollywood producer and restaurateur Victor Drai took over the hotel's basement and instituted a nouvelle French menu.

Not a scrap of Benjamin "Bugsy" Siegel's "Fabulous Flamingo" remains, but the flashy ambience still holds true. The **Flamingo Hilton Las Vegas**, 3555 Las Vegas Boulevard South, retains the original theme of "desert oasis" with a lush, 15-acre (6-hectare) tropical pool and garden area complete with swans, ducks, penguins, and

Keeping its original theme from fifty years ago, the Flamingo is still flashy and fun.

flamingos. After years of additions, the hotel now has 3530 rooms, most of them with recognizably Hilton-esque decor. Amenities range from nine restaurants to five pools, six tennis courts, a newly renovated health club, and several pricey boutiques. Most gaming tables offer low minimum bets, however, and slot junkies have more than 2,000 machines to lose from.

Adjacent to the Flamingo Hilton is tiny O'Sheas Casino, 3555 Las Vegas Boulevard South, easily overlooked amid the colossal resorts around it.

Recognizable by the blue-neon tinted pagoda architecture that stands apart on the Strip, the sprawling **Imperial Palace Hotel and Casino**, 3535 Las Vegas Boulevard South, houses 2700 rooms, 10 restaurants (including two buffets), and a 75,000-sq-ft (6,975-sq-m) casino. Aside from the gaming room, the most popular draws here are the "Legends In Concert" impersonation show and the **Imperial Palace Auto Collection**, where collectible and historic automobiles are displayed 200 at a time.

The forerunner of modern themed resorts, the **Mirage Hotel and Casino**, 3400 Las Vegas Boulevard South, shows some age when compared against the newest resorts. Still, it is attractive to both high and low rollers, owing to a lush environment (think Maui on steroids) and stylish accommodations (the pool area is particularly pleasant). The minimum bets here are a bit steep, starting at $5 for blackjack and roulette, though there is plenty of free quality entertainment once you blow your gambling budget. The Lagoon Saloon features live music in an indoor rain forest, while nine restaurants feed the hungry masses with everything from buffet fare to gourmet cuisine. To the left of the check-in desk is an incredible 20,000-gallon aquarium that's worth a look. The big attractions here are the Siegfried and Roy illusion show, the Dolphin Habitat, the Secret Garden, and the White Tiger Habitat. Fronting the hotel is the now-famous Mirage volcano that belches out flames and water to the delight of Strip pedestrians.

Harrah's Las Vegas, 3475 Las Vegas Boulevard South, recently underwent a $200-million renovation in the fall of 1997 that changed it from a Mississippi riverboat theme to a trite *Carnival* motif—a transformation that has few critics cheering. A profusion of bright colors, fiber-optic fireworks, and huge murals of international fêtes tends to put visitors on festivity over-load. It's a sizable establishment, with over 2600 accommodations and a 103,000-sq-ft (9,579-sq-m) gaming area. Seven restaurants, including the popular Range Steakhouse, offer welcome respite from the pomp and circumstance. The real fun is in The Improv comedy room.

> Most major resorts have a staff of more than 5,000.

Treasure Island at the Mirage, 3300 Las Vegas Boulevard South, offers yet more affordable elegance. From a distance, this hotel appears much like its sister resort, the Mirage. But ultimately, the $430-million Treasure Island is the lower-budget of the two, though it is not readily apparent. Detailed 18th-century Caribbean pirate exuberance—brashly carved ceilings, dark woodwork, brass adornments—is everywhere, including in the rooms. As in the Mirage, minimum betting limits start at $5 and quickly rise as the sun goes down. Outside, a blazing sea battle rages nightly between a pirate ship and British frigate, slowing pedestrian traffic to a standstill. Inside, Cirque du Soleil's "Mystère" takes the circus to new levels of sophistication. Though the whole pirate theme may seem appealing to children, this is primarily an adults-only playground—chances are the kids will have a much better time at Circus Circus.

On the site of the former Sands hotel, **The Venetian Resort Hotel-Casino**, 3355 Las Vegas Boulevard South, pushes the Italian-theming envelope. Renaissance Venice is captured via dramatic architecture and landscaping, including canals with operating gondolas and serenading gondoliers. The finished resort (some things are still being completed) will house 3036 rooms and 116,000 sq ft (10,788 sq m) of gaming. The four-level entertainment plaza includes a showroom, but the real centerpiece is the Grand Canal Shoppes, a collection of over 50 upscale shops and restaurants.

Fans of country-western music will like the **New Frontier Hotel and Casino**, 3120 Las Vegas Boulevard South. Elvis Presley played his inaugural Las Vegas show here in 1956,

A pirate's life for me: Treasure Island hosts a sea battle on the sidewalk every night.

proving that the New Frontier is not too new after all. Built long before the themed resort era with a wild-West motif, the hotel is small by contemporary standards (a "mere" 986 rooms). Amenities are spare—four restaurants, and a pool,—but the 100,000-sq-ft (9,300-sq-m) casino offers plenty of elbow room.

A Las Vegas classic, **The Desert Inn Resort and Casino**, has unfortunately closed its doors to the public. However, the golf club is still open, where you'll find the 18 holes closest to the Strip. There is talk that a bigger and better Desert Inn is in the works, but anything could happen—after all, this is Las Vegas.

Forget all that "family experience" stuff—the **Stardust Resort and Casino**, 3000 Las Vegas Boulevard South, is an adult-oriented gambling playground. With 2500 rooms and the city's most recognized signage, the Stardust is geared toward those seeking the basics: gaming, liquor, food, and topless showgirls. Over 100,000 sq ft (9300 sq m) of casino includes state-of-the-art sports betting and 2000 slot machines as well as $1 blackjack tables. There are six restaurants, and eight seperate bars handle the liquor. The Wayne Newton Theater features its namesake—six nights a week!

When it opened in 1955, the nine-story **Riviera Hotel and Casino**, 2901 Las Vegas Boulevard South, was the Strip's first high-rise, fashioned after the luxury resorts of the Côte d'Azur. Such heady days, when Liberace and Orson Welles graced the showroom, are long gone, however. Today's Riviera attracts a much more pedestrian clientele, and continuous piecemeal expansion has created a somewhat disorienting layout. There is an abundance of guest rooms (2100) and restaurants (including the upscale Kristofer's Steakhouse), as well as swimming pools, tennis

It's all fun and games at Circus-Circus, which hosts indoor acts borrowed directly from under the big top.

courts, and a small shopping area. But the real attractions beyond gambling are the four nightly live shows (a production show, a comedy club, a drag show, and a topless revue) clearly aimed at adults. Some of the showgirls involved are even immortalized in bronzed bare bottoms on the sidewalk facing the Strip.

Single-handedly responsible for pioneering the family-friendly low-roller casino some two decades ago, **Circus-Circus Hotel and Casino**, 2880 Las Vegas Boulevard South, shows signs of fatigue. The renovated lobby is classy, but one cannot expect Strip hotel rooms this cheap without a sense of compromise. Still, families will appreciate the free circus acts performed every half-hour from 11am to midnight, as well as the carnival games, arcade, and the giant indoor amusement park, **Grand Slam Canyon**. The casino

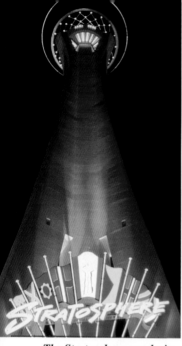

The Stratosphere may be in limbo location-wise, but it sure makes a striking stand.

area is so enormous it's separated into three areas, each connected by walkways and a monorail. Don't bother trying to find a seat to watch the circus acts—simply look up from your slot machine. Compared to the rest of the strip, the Circus-Circus has become a throwback that tends to attract low-rollers looking for some cheap thrills.

Built in 1952, the **Sahara Hotel and Casino**, 2535 Las Vegas Boulevard South, recently underwent a $100-million renovation, altering it from classic Las Vegas style to a themed Moroccan palace. The renovation took the standard route of replacing a dark and plush atmosphere with a lighter decor, and the result has been one of attractive comfort most suitable for tour groups, conventioneers, and mid-budget travelers. Close to 2000 rooms and 75,000 sq ft (6975 sq m) of gaming surround a beautiful pool area, while Speedworld offers Indy-car racing simulation. Skip the buffet, which does not get high marks. Though the casino area is anything but elegant, the minimum limits are as low as $1, and the dealers and pit bosses are far more relaxed and good-humored than those at other casinos along the Strip. If you're more interested in having fun than beating the odds, our advice is to stay and dine elsewhere, but do your gambling here.

Too far north for the Strip, too far south for Downtown, the **Stratosphere Hotel and Casino**, 2000 Las Vegas Boulevard South, and its magnificent tower struggle against the challenges of location. The complex boasts a tepid world's fair theme, but it's definitely a vast improvement over Vegas World, the universally loathed hotel it replaced. The Stratosphere's centerpiece is its 1149-ft (350-m) tower, which includes a 109th-floor observation deck (the highest in the US), an 83rd-floor revolving gourmet restaurant, and two outdoor thrill rides (the Big Shot is truly a frightening experience). Along with the requisite gaming area—which is well known for its loose slots and low-limit tables—are seven restaurants, over 40 shops, and the "American Superstars" impersonator show. Skip the $10 taxi ride from the lower Strip and hail one of the free shuttles.

DOWNTOWN

While the Las Vegas Strip eclipsed the draw of Downtown early in the city's history, the charm of Glitter Gulch has not been lost on many who visit. Both the city's oldest casino (the El Cortez) and its oldest hotel (the Golden Gate, where Las Vegas's first telephone was installed) are located Downtown, as are numerous other properties, including magnate Steve Wynn's first, the Golden Nugget.

Until recently, Fremont Street was Las Vegas's civic gathering spot, home to holiday parades and the wild-West-themed Helldorado festival. Additionally, there was once a thriving local shopping and business area here, home to

Sears, JC Penney, and numerous law and medical offices. Over time, the shopping moved to the suburbs and the attorneys moved to high-rise offices just outside the gaming area. Recently, in the face of stagnating downtown revenues, local government and business owners have explored ways to increase traffic to the famed district.

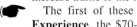   The first of these attempts was the **Fremont Street Experience**, the $70-million combined project of casino owners and the city. In 1995 Fremont Street (between Las Vegas Boulevard and Main Street) was closed to traffic and landscaped into a pedestrian mall, but the real draw of the $70 million attraction is the 90-ft (27½-m) high vaulted canopy that covers this four-block stretch. Covered with 2.1 million lights that dance to a 540,000-watt sound system, all controlled by computer, the Experience features a regular parade of amazing audio-visual shows that really wake you up. Aside from making the climate more friendly, the Experience also cleaned up the Downtown area—at least the part under its influence.

> The "Four Corners" intersection of Las Vegas Boulevard and Tropicana Avenue is one of the busiest on the planet.

The Experience has now been joined by a non-gaming entertainment complex called **Neonopolis**. Opened after much delay in 2002, the $99-million complex features the 16-screen Crown Movie Theaters, restaurants, shopping, and underground parking.

As it exists currently, the Fremont Street area is a throwback to the old days of Las Vegas gambling. Primarily due to space constraints, Downtown properties have been unable to pursue any kind of expansion, making this area representative of Las Vegas in its purest form. House gambling rules are generally more flexible, allowing for both

Four blocks of fantastic audio-visual effects draw visitors out of the casinos and on to Fremont Street.

lower minimum bets and higher limits (sometimes even no-limit gaming). Additionally, there is a certain rough quality to Downtown, an experience different than that offered at the shiny new Strip resorts. Do not mistake this edginess for danger; the Fremont Street Experience has done quite a bit to improve the safety of the area beneath the canopy, sometimes drawing the ire of civil rights and free speech activists.

Main Street Station, 200 North Main Street, is perhaps Las Vegas's best-kept secret. Just north of the Fremont Street Experience, this Victorian-styled casino fulfills the promise of the exterior architecture and gas-fired street lamps with an astoundingly detailed interior filled with expensive antiques. Unlike other casinos, the Main Street's theme showcases genuine articles, a carved Scottish fireplace and Teddy Roosevelt's Pullman car among them. Dining includes the upscale Pullman Grille for steak and seafood, as well as the Triple 7 Brewpub for handcrafted ales and wood-fired pizza.

The name of the **California Hotel and Casino**, 12 Ogden Avenue, in this case, says very little. The California is an off-Fremont hotel-casino that spends most of its marketing budget in Hawaii, attracting native Hawaiians by the planeload (the state's inhabitants make up 85 percent of the casino's business). Consequently, the decor offers a taste of the South Seas, while the four restaurant menus include Hawaiian specialties. There is also a Hawaiian specialty store on premise, and 781 modestly priced rooms geared toward the budget traveler.

> **Las Vegas employs 12,560 maids and housekeeping attendants.**

The **Lady Luck Casino Hotel**, 206 North Third Street, is a collection of neon, mirrors, and brass, going a long way toward preserving the glitzy Las Vegas of old. Close to 800 rooms, especially in the two newer towers, are very comfortable. The hotel-casino has two Downtown rarities: a showroom, staging a production magic show, and a pool. Four restaurants serve guests, including the gourmet Burgundy Room, a member of the exclusive Chaîne des Rôtisseurs association.

The **Las Vegas Club Hotel and Casino**, 18 East Fremont Street, one of the oldest casinos in Las Vegas, marks the beginning of the newest Downtown attraction, the Fremont Experience canopy. Explore 40,000 sq ft (3720 sq m) of gaming with some of the most liberal house rules in town. The modest theming here features a widely dispersed exhibition of sports memorabilia, as well as card dealers dressed in jersey-like uniforms. The hotel tower was added in 1980 and features 410 affordable, comfortable rooms. There are also three casual restaurants.

A smoky, 1970s environment anchored by a bus station and a defunct rail station, **Jackie Gaughan's Plaza Hotel and Casino**, 1 Main Street—located at the west end of the Fremont Street Experience canopy—has always been a maverick hotel-casino. With just over 1000 rooms and a 75,000-sq-ft (6975-sq-m) gaming area that includes penny slot machines, the Plaza attracts an interesting mix of friendly gamblers and seniors. The showroom offers on-again, off-again, campy, adult-oriented revues.

Cinemas and Simulators

Cinema Ride. 11am–11pm daily, until midnight Friday and Saturday. $8–$16. Short but fairly entertaining 3-D motion simulator movies; the high cost is more palatable with a multiple-admission ticket. *The Forum Shops at Caesars Palace, 3500 Las Vegas Boulevard South; Tel. (702) 369-4008.*

IMAX Theatre. 9am–10:30pm daily. $7.50–$8.50. IMAX films are always dazzling. *Luxor Hotel and Casino, 3900 Las Vegas Boulevard South; Tel. (702) 262-4000.*

In Search of the Obelisk Motion Simulator. 9am–11pm daily. $5. Less expensive and superior to Cinema Ride. *Luxor Hotel and Casino, 3900 Las Vegas Boulevard South; Tel. (702) 262-4000.*

Omnimax Theatre. 2–10pm daily, screenings hourly. $5–$7. The effects in this film are very good, but the 3-D can make some viewers nauseous. *Caesars Palace Hotel and Casino, 3570 Las Vegas Boulevard South; Tel. (702) 731-7110.*

Speedworld Indy Racing Simulator. 10am–10:30pm daily, until midnight Friday and Sunday. $8. Thrill to the experience of racing a scaled-down Indy Car replica through a harrowingly realistic virtual race. *Sahara Hotel and Casino, 2535 Las Vegas Boulevard South; Tel. (702) 737-2111.*

Perhaps the only bed-and-breakfast experience in Las Vegas, the classic San Francisco-styled **Golden Gate Hotel and Casino**, One Fremont Street, has stood here since 1906. The charming operation is the city's oldest hotel, the home of its first telephone, and the initial purveyor of the classic shrimp cocktail. Its 106 small (100 sq ft/9 sq m) but elegant rooms with plaster walls and mahogany doors hearken back to another era, and its coffee shop is an unusually classy Downtown experience. Piano players entertain with infectious ragtime.

The only Downtown hotel-casino without a neon sign, the 1946 **Golden Nugget**, 129 East Fremont Street, was remodeled as Steve Wynn's first hotel project in 1987. Metropolitan elegance supersedes the surrounding glitz. Guests, greeted by uniformed doormen, enter a gilded lobby full of marble and crystal. The 1,907 guest rooms and misted pool area landscaped with palms are fancy enough to have earned top ratings.

The historic Golden Nugget was the first renovation project of Las Vegas entrepreneur Steve Wynn.

The Golden Nugget showroom offers headliners and production shows; there are five restaurants as well, including a top-notch mid-priced buffet and two gourmet dining rooms.

A blinding neon landmark since 1966, the **Four Queens Hotel and Casino**, 202 Fremont Street, today mainly attracts older guests, many of whom are repeat customers. A 12-seat blackjack table (the world's largest) and a giant slot machine draw players to the 60,000-sq-ft (5580-sq-m) casino. The seven hundred rooms of earth-tone decor are pleasant and affordable. Its four restaurants include Hugo's Cellar, an always-busy classic Las Vegas gourmet room with a winning wine list.

The **Fitzgerald's Casino Hotel**, 301 Fremont Street, is Las Vegas's low-roller haven, offering an astounding 1000 slot machines within 42,000 sq ft (3906 sq m) of gaming space. Once the tallest building in Nevada at 34 stories, the Fitzgerald's 650 rooms offer great views of the city and mountains. Accommodations are of the national chain variety and priced accordingly, as are the four restaurants and numerous bars.

Founded by old-school gambler Benny Binion, **Binion's Horseshoe Hotel and Casino**, 128 Fremont Street, may be the most traditional gambling joint left in town. Its flocked-wallpaper-and-velvet-drape ambiance ensconces gaming tables that offer the highest betting limits in the world, including no-limit gaming. Additionally, the Horseshoe hosts the $1-million World Series of Poker each year. The Binions are ranchers as well, and premium beef can be had in both the casual coffee shop and the upscale Ranch Steak House. Don't miss the free opportunity to have your photo taken next to a million dollars.

Las Vegas's first high-rise, built in 1956, and famous for launching Wayne Newton's career, **Sam Boyd's Fremont Hotel and Casino**, 200 East Fremont Street, today shows signs of wear. The hotel no longer has a showroom, but 452 modest

Saved from the scrap heap, this electric cowgirl now graces Fremont Street.

guest rooms help accommodate the Hawaiian travelers who frequent the place and its 32,000 sq ft (2976 sq m) of gaming. The Fremont's block-long signage is among the principal reasons Downtown turns night into day, and the Second Street Grill is a hidden gem, featuring Pacific Rim specialties.

As Las Vegas experienced record growth and continued a trend towards the implosion of its older resorts, a desire arose to preserve some of the city's history. Neon signage is perhaps the single most recognizable icon of Las Vegas. Thus, the **Neon Museum** has assumed the responsibility of raising funds to restore some of the rusting signs from the past and display them in their intended glory. Recently, five signs were installed on posts in the Fremont Street Experience in a rare example of public art.

Unrivaled for its continuous parade of low-stakes gamblers and their related atmosphere, the **El Cortez Hotel and Casino**, 600 Fremont Street (built in 1941), is the city's oldest operating casino. Unabashedly proletarian, the gaming area is filled with smoke and the cheap perfume worn by the ragtag old-timers who frequent its slot machines. The relatively large 80,000-sq-ft (7440-sq-m) casino features absurdly low limits, while dining rooms offer ridiculously cheap food. Semi-annual lotteries based on social security numbers are held for $50,000 prizes. There are 402 rooms at low prices; in the tower, you will get a bit more than you pay for.

Local culture can be sampled at the **Arts Factory** complex, 101–109 East Charleston Boulevard (Tel. 702/676-1111). An old warehouse converted into exhibit spaces and artists' studios, this place is a touch of SoHo in Sin City and the linchpin of a growing Downtown arts scene. Inside are a mix of commercial and nonprofit galleries offering a variety of exhibitions: avant-garde modern art in the **Contemporary Arts Collective** (Tel. 702/382-3886); local and regional artists in the **Smallworks Gallery** (Tel. 702/388-8857); and more mainstream artistic offerings in the **George L. Sturman Fine Arts Gallery** (Tel. 702/384-2615).

BEYOND THE STRIP

Las Vegas has been described as "Des Moines with casinos," and to a certain extent that is true—beyond the glitter of the Strip, the quality of attractions pales somewhat. But there are still intriguing stops worth a visitor's time and effort. And while most hotel-casinos and resorts are concentrated along the Strip and within the Downtown area, some are found just off the Strip. To the west are recently developed resort corridors off both Flamingo Road and Tropicana Avenue. These areas consist primarily of light industrial development with sparse housing or apartments nearby. To the east is the convention area of Paradise Road, offering—in addition to traditional hotel-casinos—a spate of non-gaming business-oriented hotels as well as a developing restaurant row. Further south, along a stretch of the industrialized Boulder Highway between Las Vegas and Henderson called Boulder Strip, are a number of hotel-casinos, ranging from questionable to sensational. Below are the highlights of these off-Strip properties and attractions.

West of the Strip

Offering a combination of entertainment and gaming, the **Gold Coast Hotel and Casino**, 4000 West Flamingo Road, fulfills many traditional Las Vegas expectations. On site is a 72-lane bowling center, a lounge with live karaoke, and a dance hall that regularly features live big-band, swing, and rockabilly music. Dining rooms are varied, inexpensive, and good, while a twin theater (with unbelievably cheap concessions) screens an alternating parade of blockbusters and festival films. The true casino draw is in the huge number of video poker machines, which attract mainly locals, despite the 740 hotel rooms.

The showy façade of the **Orleans Hotel and Casino**, 4500 W. Tropicana Avenue, is a bit misleading and overbearing; once you enter, the décor is rather subtle. The casino is more akin to a warehouse than the Big Easy, but the 50-ft (15-m) ceilings do well to eradicate the typical smoky, claustrophobic atmosphere. A 72-lane bowling center and 12-screen cinema attract locals, while the eight casual restaurants and 827-seat showroom (staging second tier or aging acts) attract anyone seeking quality on a budget. Rooms are spacious and among the city's best bargains.

The **Palace Station Hotel and Casino**, 2411 West Sahara Avenue, was the first Station casino, and, despite its proximity to the Strip, the one that started the locals-hangout trend. The atmosphere is crowded, smoky, and loud, owing to the 2200 slot machines. The world's largest slot jackpot— worth $27.6 million—was won here in 1998 by a 23-year Las Vegas resident. Still, the 1028 comfortable rooms signify a willingness to court travelers, and five casual restaurants, including trendsetting cook stations at the Feast Buffet, offer excellent bargains.

The **Rio Suites Hotel and Casino**, 3700 West Flamingo Road, offers such a variety of quality mid-priced amenities that it has received international acclaim. A recent addition raised the room total to 2556, and the standard accommodations are among the city's largest. Also added were **Masquerade Village**—a Carnivale-themed collection of gaming, retail outlets, and restaurants (including Napa, one of Nevada's best)—and the **Voodoo Lounge**, a top-floor cocktail lounge with citywide views. The casino floor, lorded over by serious-looking pit bosses wearing laughably gaudy tropical wear, is usually packed with both locals and tourists, especially on weekends. Five-dollar minimum bets are standard. After the last performance of the night the showroom morphs into the Club Rio disco, which offers late-night dancing.

The Convention Center and Paradise Road Area

For all its reputation as a vacation hot-spot, Las Vegas has also enjoyed tremendous success as a major convention destination. Every week companies, industries, and lifestyle organizations arrive en masse from all over the world to mix business with pleasure. How vital are such trade shows to the city economy?

Millions of conventioneers from all over the world converge here, at the Las Vegas Convention Center.

Enough so that most Las Vegas resorts have elaborate convention facilities, as do suburbs such as Henderson.

The king, however, is the **Las Vegas Convention Center**. With 760,000 sq ft (70,680 sq m) of exhibit space and a whopping 91 meeting rooms, this complex ranks as the largest single-story convention floor in the United States. What's more, it is within walking distance of more than 50,000 hotel rooms.

The **Las Vegas Hilton Hotel and Casino**, 3000 South Paradise Road—located next to the Convention Center—is paradise to those accustomed to large-scale resorts that cater to one's every need. You could easily stay here a week and never find reason to leave. Public areas are gracious and expensively decorated, and the already plush 3174 guest rooms recently underwent renovation. Amenities include a spa, six lighted tennis courts, 12 restaurants, and a showroom and lounge featur-

Conventional Wisdom

Despite its enormous size, many conventions still spill out of the Las Vegas Convention Center to adjacent hotel facilities, most notably the Las Vegas Hilton. Electronics industry shows in particular—COMDEX and the Consumer Electronics Show every fall and winter—tend to be especially sprawling. Other significant conventions include gatherings of the construction-equipment giants, automobile accessory marketers, fashion companies, and even pizza-equipment industries.

The obvious financial up-side of such an influx of conventioneers is somewhat offset by the equally obvious down-side: snarled traffic, inflated room rates, and packed attractions. Some merchants—and most taxi drivers—complain that conventioneers are less free-spending than vacationers. It all falls on deaf bureaucratic ears, however, as city planners continue to woo convention trade by expanding its main Convention Center and adding new ones throughout the valley.

ing top talent. Hilton highlights are a sports betting floor of amazing dimensions—30,500 sq ft (2836 sq m)—and **Star Trek: The Experience**, a permanent high-tech attraction featuring futuristic gaming, dining, and its centerpiece interactive amusement ride. Because of its close proximity to the Las Vegas Convention building, the Hilton's occupancy—not to mention its rates—rises quickly during large conventions, so be sure to make the proper inquiries before booking a room.

One of the more notable hotels in Las Vegas not located on the strip is the **Hard Rock Hotel and Casino**, 4455 Paradise Road. A surprising exercise in casual elegance considering its theme, this experiment aimed at the younger market has resulted in a rebirth of the glory days of Las Vegas. If you're wondering where all the hip and pretty people hang out, this is it. Music memorabilia perched above hardwood flooring surrounds the handsome casino—slot machine handles, for example, are shaped like Fender Stratocaster guitar necks—while performers of every genre fill the 1200-seat club-style

> If you want to make sure your vacation doesn't coincide with a major convention, see Calendar of Events on page 74.

showroom. Dining includes the trendy Mr. Lucky's 24/7 and the upscale Mortoni's. A lush pool area greets sunbathers, and rooms are spacious and very tasteful. Recent expansion has doubled the property's amenities; hopefully it will not destroy this hotel's renowned intimacy.

Boulder Highway

Where Fremont Street becomes the Boulder Highway sits the **Showboat Hotel, Casino, and Bowling Center**, 2800 Fremont Street, a recently remodeled New Orleans-themed casino. Featuring the world's largest bowling facility with 106 lanes open 24 hours, the Showboat also hosts an annual January PBA tournament. Bingo is a big draw as well, owing to a 1200-seat parlor. Four restaurants, an RV park, and 60,000 sq ft (5580 sq m) of gaming help attract guests to this slightly off-the-path location, as do the 500 small but comfortable rooms.

The Station Hotel and Casino chain has done well offering a moderately priced version of the inclusive upscale resort. At **Boulder Station Hotel and Casino**, 4111 Boulder Highway, guests can enjoy an 11-screen imaginatively themed movie theater complex, while children will love KidsQuest, a huge supervised indoor play area. The hotel-casino's Railhead Saloon lounge, with 750 seats, stages a variety of world-class niche entertainers. The property features five restaurants, a sprawling buffet, and 300 modestly priced rooms.

At **Sam's Town Hotel and Casino**, 5111 Boulder Highway, as is traditionally the case in casinos aiming at the local market, the enormous gaming floor (some 130,000 sq ft/12,090 sq m) greatly outpaces the 650 available rooms. A country-western theme permeates—including a huge Western Emporium—and the casino is typically loud and smoky. However, the range and caliber of the amenities is completely unexpected. There are nine casual restaurants of surprisingly good quality and 56 lanes of high-tech bowling. The real treat is the nine-story atrium over an indoor park, complete with live trees, running water, and footpaths.

Elsewhere Around Las Vegas

Liberace may no longer be with us, but Mr. Showmanship's absolutely fabulous cars, gilded pianos, and indescribable costumes can still be seen at the **Liberace Museum**, 1775 E. Tropicana Avenue (Tel. 702/798-5595), snuggled in a mall a short drive from the Strip. The jewel of the collection may in fact be a fake jewel—a 50-pound rhinestone, said to be the world's largest. If you have even an inkling to visit this sensational shrine to one of the world's most popular entertainers, do so—it's worth the drive.

Other institutions dedicated to Las Vegas history include the **Nevada State Museum and Historical Society**, 700 Twin Lakes Drive (Tel. 702/486-5205), and the **Clark County Heritage Museum**, 1830 South Boulder Highway

---

Museums and Exhibits

Bellagio Gallery of Fine Art. 10am–10pm daily. $12; audio tour an additional $4. This small collection is interesting, if not world-class. *Bellagio Hotel and Casino, 3600 Las Vegas Boulevard South; Tel. (702) 693-7111.*

Dolphin Habitat and Secret Garden. 11am–7pm, daily. $10, children under 10 free. The small zoo is beautifully landscaped, the dolphin exhibit is fun. *Mirage Hotel and Casino, 3400 Las Vegas Boulevard South; Tel. (702) 791-7111.*

Imperial Palace Auto Collection. 9:30am–9:30pm daily. $3–$6.95; under 3 free. A relatively inexpensive and interesting exhibit (especially for car buffs). *Imperial Palace Hotel and Casino, 3535 Las Vegas Boulevard South; Tel. (702) 731-3311.*

Liberace Museum. Monday–Saturday 10am–5pm; Sunday 1–5pm; $8.00 adults, $5 senior and students, under 12 free. A museum devoted to "Mr. Showmanship"; though off the beaten path, it is worth the drive. *1775 E. Tropicana Avenue; Tel. (702) 798-5595.*

Stratosphere Tower and Observation Deck. Sun–Thurs 10am–1am, until 2am Fri, Sat, and holidays. $6. The tallest structure in Nevada offers a great view. *Stratosphere Hotel and Casino, 2000 Las Vegas Boulevard South; Tel. (702) 380-7777.*

(Tel. 702/455-7955). The state museum has a mammoth display—that is, a wooly mammoth, of the variety that used to live in ancient Nevada, one of many archaeological exhibits on view. The Heritage Museum, a short drive away in Henderson, features several intact structures from different periods of local history, as well as various cultural exhibits. Meanwhile, visitors to the **Mormon Fort** (southeast corner of Las Vegas Boulevard and Washington; Tel. 702-486-3511) can see remnants of the city's oldest building, a fort built by original Mormon settlers in 1855.

Across town to the west is the **Las Vegas Art Museum** (Tel. 702/360-8000). Actually a museum space attached to the Sahara West Library, it is quite large, having been designed to exacting Smithsonian specifications. Curators

Liberace had a flair for flash and a taste for fantastic old cars, which you can ogle at his eponymous museum.

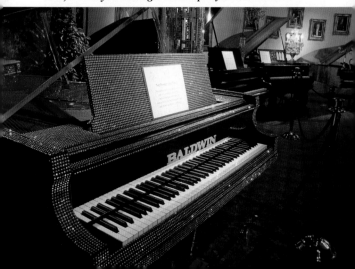

schedule a mix of local and touring shows, often including work by recognized masters.

The **University of Nevada at Las Vegas** (UNLV) and the **Community College of Southern Nevada** have been unofficial outposts of beyond-the-Neon culture since their inception. UNLV's sprawling urban campus (4505 South Maryland Parkway; Tel. 702/895-3011) has quite a collection of interesting sights and venues. The Barrick Museum (Tel. 702/895-3381) is a natural history museum and also mounts some excellent exhibitions. Just outside the entrance is the campus Xeric Garden, a landscaped sampling of desert plants in a beautiful setting. The Donna Beam Fine Arts Gallery (Tel. 702/895-3893) is a spacious hall exhibiting the work of students as well as professionals. Also on campus: the Artemus Ham Concert Hall (Tel. 702/895-3801), featuring classical, rock, and theatrical performances, and the Thomas and Mack Center, an 18,000-seat arena hosting everything from hockey to rodeos and musical events. On the Community College Campus (3200 East Cheyenne Avenue; Tel. 702/651-4000) the city's only **planetarium** features nightly shows of both Omni-screen films and programs about the heavens (Tel. 702/651-4759).

Though not providing the same ritzy atmosphere of the Strip or Downtown Las Vegas, neighborhood casinos often feature reduced minimum betting and a smaller, more accessible atmosphere. Travelers who seek less pressure and do not require an elaborate atmosphere may even want to stay away from the tourist areas; the hotel-casinos described here also offer a good—and sometimes wonderful—alternative.

Built around the former Charleston Heights Lanes (but no longer offering bowling), **Arizona Charlie's**, 740 South

The Reserve takes advantage of Henderson's wide-open spaces to assume the sprawl of an African game reserve.

Decatur Boulevard (Tel. 702/258-5200 or 1-800-342-2695), is a no-frills neighborhood gambling joint. The gaming floor is always active, while the entertainment runs from touring country-western singers to classic rock bands. The lounge usually stages an above-average local blues or country band, and the occasional pro and semi-pro boxing match takes place on the premises, just like in the old days. Four restaurants include China Charlie's, an inexpensive Asian favorite; 200 rooms provide modest accommodations.

Sure, the **Santa Fe Hotel and Casino**, 4949 North Rancho Drive (Tel. 702/658-4900 or 1-800-457-2882), has guest rooms—200 to be exact. It also has 50,000 sq ft (4650 sq m) of gaming, a 60-lane bowling center, three bars and two lounges. But what truly separates the Santa Fe from any other Las Vegas hotel-casino—neighborhood or otherwise—is its ice-skating arena. Pros and amateurs alike share the ice on a daily basis. The other major attraction is Suzette's, a dining room offering what has been called the best French cuisine in town.

If neighborhood casinos must exist, the **Sunset Station**, 1301 West Sunset Road, should be the benchmark. The Mediterranean interior is stunning, especially within the Gaudi Bar. A 13-screen cinema often serves as the valley's art house, and the major video arcade and KidsQuest indoor play area make this a family mainstay. Thirteen restaurants range from fast to feast. Sunset Station, with 80,000 sq ft (7440 sq m) of gaming and 448 rooms, is located across from a major shopping mecca, including the Galleria mall.

Cleverly themed as an African game reserve but rather small and unassuming, **The Reserve**, 777 West Lake Mead Drive (Tel. 702/567-7777 or 1-888-899-7770), is the latest neighborhood casino to enter Henderson. The casino offers 37,000 sq ft (3441 sq m) of gaming, a 300-seat bingo room, and three cocktail lounges. Family amenities are limited to six restaurants, including Tusk, whose atmosphere entertains both adults and children. The 224 rooms are comfortable and affordable.

A short drive to the eastern side of the valley can easily turn into a tasty treat-journey with a stop in nearby Henderson: at the **Ethel M. Chocolate Factory**, 2 Cactus Garden Drive (Tel. 702/433-2500). At the site you can watch the plant's signature products being manufactured and load up on free samples. Particularly notable at Ethel M.—aside from workers turning out Milky Way, Three Musketeer's, and Snickers bars—is the company's garden of desert plants, one of the most extensive in town. To get to Henderson, drive east on Tropicana Avenue, make a right on Mountain Vista, then continue on 2 miles (3 km) to Sunset Way; from there you will turn left into the Green Valley Business Park, where you will find Ethel M., a good place to begin.

Farther afield, **The Regent Las Vegas**, Summerlin Parkway at Rampart (Tel. 702/869-7500), is a plush, upscale country club and spa comprised of two unique resorts located on a championship golf course. The Regent Grand Spa features a 40,000-sq-ft (3720-sq-m) spa. The Grand Palms tower is set among 1000 palms in a garden environment. There are 541 rooms. The complex, with 50,000 sq ft

Thrill Rides and Theme Parks

Big Shot and High Roller Roller Coaster. 10am–1am daily, until 2am Friday and Saturday (weather permitting). $9 High Roller; $11 Big Shot; $15 gets you both rides and the trip up the tower. These two outdoor thrill rides high atop the Stratosphere Tower are actually thrilling. *Stratosphere Hotel and Casino, 2000 Las Vegas Boulevard South; Tel. (702) 380-7777*.

Grand Slam Canyon Amusement Park. 10am–6pm daily, until midnight Friday and Saturday; Sunday 10–8. Entrance is free, rides $3–5 each; day passes are available. This small amusement park is popular with kids. *Circus-Circus Hotel and Casino, 2880 Las Vegas Boulevard South; Tel. (702) 734-0410*.

Manhattan Express Roller Coaster. 10am–11pm daily, until 11:30pm Friday and Saturday (weather permitting). $10. This roller coaster, which you can observe speeding within the hotel itself, is worth the hefty price tag. *New York-New York Hotel and Casino, 3790 Las Vegas Boulevard South; Tel. (702) 740-6969*.

MGM Theme Park and Sky Screamer. Open spring and summer only, 11am–7pm daily (weather permitting). Park admission prices vary; Sky Screamer costs $25–45. The small theme park is somewhat disappointing, but can be diverting for children. *MGM Grand Hotel and Casino, 3799 Las Vegas Boulevard South; Tel. (702) 891-7777*.

Star Trek: The Experience. 11am–11pm daily. $19.95. This attraction features a very good motion simulator ride and good special effects. *Las Vegas Hilton Hotel and Casino, 3000 South Paradise Road; Tel. (702) 732-5111*.

(4650 sq m) of gaming and six restaurants, is targeted at travelers accustomed to other high-rent desert resorts. To get to Summerlin, drive west on Sahara Boulevard about 6 miles (9½ km) to Rampart. Turn right (north) and continue about 2 miles (3 km).

EXCURSIONS

Hoover Dam and Lake Mead

There is much to do within relatively easy driving distance of Las Vegas, from recreation to sightseeing. Easily the top draw is **Hoover Dam**, responsible for Las Vegas's first major crowd (of 20,000), who attended its 1935 dedication. Long after its completion, the dam remains an awe-inspiring sight, living up to its old billing as the "Eighth Wonder of the World."

A dizzying 725 ft (526 m) high, this engineering marvel straddles the Nevada-Arizona border a half-hour south of Las Vegas on US 93. A posh visitor center offers facts and displays regarding the massive structure. Frequent tours lead the curious into the tunnels and electricity-generating turbines within the dam.

The man-made result of Hoover Dam, **Lake Mead** (Tel. 702/293-8990) offers more than 500 miles (800 km) of shoreline in the midst of a 1.5-million-acre (607,000-hectare) national recreation area. A popular recreation spot for locals and visitors alike, the lake—America's largest man-made body of water—is open all year (peak usage month is June). Available activities include swimming, boating, fishing, water-skiing, self-guided hiking, camping, and picnicking. Boats can be rented at the Lake Mead Marina (Tel. 702/293-3484) or the Echo Bay Marina (Tel. 702/394-4000). If a cruise is more your style, the Desert

Princess Lake Mead Cruises paddle-wheel boat offers breakfast and dinner rides (Tel. 702/293-6180). The same company schedules trips around the lake via Jet Skis, as well as a jet-boat excursion down the Colorado River to the edge of the Grand Canyon.

The lake is best reached through Boulder City, a half-hour drive south from Las Vegas. A few miles past the city you will find the Alan Bible Visitors Center. Many daily bus tours leave Las Vegas for Hoover Dam from here, for those visitors without access to an automobile.

Boulder City

Boulder City itself is an anomaly in Nevada—a city that rejects gaming and discourages excess growth. Its small-town feel is quaint and charming by the standards of booming suburban southern Nevada. The heart of the town is a historic square, fronted by 1930s-era buildings such as the **Boulder Dam Hotel** and the **Boulder Dam Theatre**. The hotel is a hotel in name only; rooms are not available. But

the building does house several galleries, shops, and an attractive restaurant. The town is home to several art galleries and antiques shops; call the chamber of commerce at (702) 293-2034 for details. Also worth seeing: the **Hoover Dam Museum**, well-stocked with artifacts

Hoover Dam is a wonder on the outside and quite interesting from within.

A little tired of being indoors? Take a break from the slots and get some sun at Lake Mead.

from the building of the dam and the founding of Boulder City. In the fall, several festivals, including Art In The Park and Damboree (a celebration of the town's heritage), entice thousands to make the trek from Las Vegas. Take US 93 south about 25 miles (40 km) from Las Vegas; Hoover Dam is an additional 7 miles (11 km).

Ghost Towns

While not technically a ghost town—a few dozen people still live there—**Goodsprings** certainly has the feel of one. The functioning homes are surrounded by mill foundations and abandoned mine operations left over from better days. The hamlet's chief attraction is the Pioneer Saloon, a popular joint built in 1913 and still the country's largest stamped-metal building. Head south from Las Vegas on Interstate 15 and turn at the tiny town of Jean.

For an authentic ghost town, see **Rhyolite**, located 126 miles (200 km) northwest of Las Vegas on US 95. Once Nevada's second-largest city, thanks to a 1904 gold strike, remnants of those glory days can be seen in the still-intact Tonopah–Las Vegas Railroad depot and other structures in varying states of dilapidation. A top attraction is the "bottle house," built of 50,000 glass bottles, a common practice in the old days of scarce building supplies. Just outside of town is an improbable cluster of large sculptures by Belgian artists. The pieces include Albert Szukalski's "Last Supper" (a three-dimensional re-creation of the da Vinci masterpiece using plaster ghosts in place of the Disciples), a 28-ft (8½ m) miner, a penguin made of metal, and a 25-ft (7½-m) female nude built of cinder blocks.

Valley Of Fire

Fifty miles (80 km) northeast of Las Vegas via I-15 (watch for the Valley of Fire exit, State Route 169), **Valley of Fire**

Bike the loop, climb a rock, take a picnic, or watch the birds at Red Rock Canyon.

State Park (Tel. 702/397-2088) is a spectacular, Mars-like landscape of erosion-sculpted, brilliant red sandstone. The park features Indian petroglyphs dating to 300 B.C., most accessible via light hiking. Atlatyl Rock has a stairway to the carvings, while the glyphs at Mouse's Tank require an easy quarter-mile (½ km) trek. For the car-bound, there is a 6-mile (9½ km) scenic loop through White Domes, a stunning vista of sandstone formations that were once the bottom of an inland sea. There are also some picnic areas and a handful of overnight camping sites. If you visit in late spring or summer, go early; afternoon temperatures approach 120° F (49° C). Winter temperatures reach freezing at night.

Red Rock Canyon

Red Rock Canyon National Recreation Area, a half-hour drive west of Downtown Las Vegas via Charleston Boulevard, is a dramatic vista of mountains and colorful sheer rock faces. Actually more than a single canyon, it is a 13-mile (21-km) ridge with canyons eroded into its flanks. First stop: the Red Rock Visitors Center (Tel. 702/363-1921), which has archaeological displays and dioramas depicting the lives of Indians who once lived there.

Starting at the center, the scenic loop meanders through the area's stunning topography. If you drive the loop, pay careful attention and watch out for bicyclists. Picnicking spaces are plentiful, as are hiking trails of varying levels of difficulty. During migratory seasons, bird watchers can have a field day. Not surprisingly, the canyon is one of the nation's top rock-climbing sites, with an almost endless variety of ascents. Be warned: novices should stick to the levels of hiking or rock climbing they can handle. Many times each year, rescuers are called to the canyon to help lost or injured visitors. Entrance to the Canyon is $5 per vehicle.

Mount Charleston

For a cool break from the desert, try 12,000-ft (3658-m) Mount Charleston, 40 minutes north of Las Vegas on US 95. Two areas command your attention: Kyle Canyon and Lee Canyon. Kyle is home to scenic Cathedral Rock, Mary Jane Falls, and Big Falls, all accessible by trail (Cathedral Rock requires a three-hour trek, however). Lee Canyon is home to a ski and snowboarding resort. The mountain features numerous scenic overlooks and picnicking sites. The ranger station on Kyle Canyon Road (Tel. 702/872-5486) can provide maps and advice.

The Grand Canyon

There are several noteworthy national parks within driving distance of Las Vegas. The most famous, of course, is the **Grand Canyon** of Arizona. The North Rim is 280 miles (448 km) east of Las Vegas, the South Rim (the more commercialized of the two), 260 miles (416 km). There are no connecting bridges.

The 277-mile- (443-km-) long natural wonder, more than 5000 ft (1524 m) deep at some points, makes for an ideal day trip. The South Rim, accessible by Interstate 40, is the most visited area of the park; the North Rim—arrived at by Interstate 15 through St. George, Utah—receives a fraction of the traffic. What to do while you are there? What not to do! There are several driving trails with numerous scenic overlooks. There are also walking trails along the rim, although be warned: as one visitors' guide says, they are "narrow and close to the edge."

For the active traveler, the park offers backpacking, rafting, and mule-back descents into the canyon. Note: back-country hiking requires an advance permit; hikes down to the river generally take two days or more, returning twice as long. For the more sedentary, there are historic sites to visit, star-gazing, bird-watching, and, of course, enough spectacular scenery to keep

The Grand Canyon, carved through the ages by the flow of the Colorado River, is less than a day's drive away.

the eyes busy. If you wish to travel down into the canyon, you must plan far ahead of time; it would be wise to make arrangements several months to a year in advance.

If you prefer not to drive, several Las Vegas-based tour operators offer air and bus tours of the canyon. Call the Las Vegas Convention and Visitors Authority at (702) 892-0711.

As for weather, both rims get snow in winter, and even summer evenings may be chilly. Due to weather conditions, the North Rim is open only May to October. Down in the canyon, more desert-like conditions prevail, with summer afternoons approaching 120° F (49° C). For more information, call (520) 638-7864.

Death Valley

Death Valley, presumed resting place of many a doomed 49er—actually, only one is known to have died there—is 145 miles (232 km) west of Las Vegas. It can be reached by US 95 northwest or Interstate 15 south to Baker, California. Popular destinations in this desert include Furnace Creek (which, with a gas station, hotels, and golf course, is the only dot of civilization on the map), and the improbable Scotty's Castle, a lavish building erected by the legendary Death Valley Scotty in the absolute middle of nowhere. The Death Valley National Park Visitors Center (Tel. 760/786-2331) has maps and more information.

Zion and Bryce Canyon National Parks

Northeast, in Utah, are the spectacular Zion and Bryce Canyon national parks. Just 155 miles (248 km) from Las Vegas, Zion (Tel. 435/772-3256) offers a smorgasbord of natural wonders, including stark rock formations, sheer cliff faces, waterfalls, and lush forests. The park, accessible year-round, is laced with hiking trails and scenic drives.

Further north—210 miles (336 km) from Las Vegas—is Bryce Canyon, an amazing series of natural amphitheaters scooped from the edge of the Paunsagunt Plateau by the Paria River. Bryce (Tel. 435/834-5322) is renowned for its colorful formations of sculptured rock—pinnacles, pedestals, fins, and spires. Sinking Ship, Thor's Hammer, and Natural Bridge, an awesome rock arch, are just some of the spectacular sights.

Great Basin National Park

A longer drive—five hours—will bring you to Great Basin National Park (Tel. 775/234-7331) along the Nevada-Utah state line. Is it worth the trek? That depends on how you feel about 77,000 acres (31,160 hectares) of rugged back country, groves of ancient bristlecone pine trees, and Lehman Caves, the premier limestone cavern system in the western United States. To find the nation's 49th national park, head north using interstates 93 and 50, and state highways 487 and 488.

WHAT TO DO

To say that Las Vegas is a non-traditional city barely begins to hint at what a trip here will foretell. To say that gambling is the number one revenue source for business and taxes, and therefore has an immeasurable impact on the nature of the city, would be stating the obvious. Yet gambling is only half the story.

The other half is where the gamblers come from, how they arrive here, and how they are served once they arrive. Gambling and entertainment may be the attractions, but tourism and service is the industry.

Las Vegas reaps the rewards and suffers the losses of a metropolis of over one million residents whose primary industry is tourism. This existence makes the traditional travelers'

In Las Vegas, there will never be a lack of things to do—or just to look at, for that matter.

A little magic with your meal? There's a new surprise with every experience in Las Vegas.

definitions of "what to do" and "where to go" difficult to delineate. In Las Vegas, the two overlap, often to the point of indistinctness. Casinos and resorts and gambling and entertainment: where does one stop and the other begin? The answer is that they are interrelated and interdependent.

Until relatively recently, entertainment industries in Las Vegas were aimed primarily at the visitor. For the most part, if locals wanted to experience any kind of entertainment or leisure time, they would likely visit one of the same establishments as the tourists.

With the overwhelming population explosion that started in the late 1980s came an unspoken demand from the locals for more traditional, off-Strip experiences, thus sparking a growth in local culture and amenities. Today, that process is still young but steadily evolving. Locals and visitors are each feeling their way along a new path for experiencing Las Vegas, one that combines the expected attractions of the gaming and tourism industry with those types of independent cultural amenities found in a more traditional city of its size. The happy result is a combination of the expected and the unexpected.

GAMBLING

Since 1931, when gambling was officially legalized in Nevada after 22 years of prohibition, it has been used to promote the city to travelers. Without question, the primary allure of Las Vegas—despite the resorts, restaurants, showrooms, and shopping malls—is the fact that one can legally place bets on games of chance and sporting events. Make no mistake: the times may be changing, but without gambling, there would be no Forum Shops, no pirate ships, no Bellagio Gallery of Fine Art.

Most of the gambling in Las Vegas is concentrated along the Strip, where nearly twenty major casinos in excess of 100,000 sq ft (9300 sq m) beckon passers-by to lighten their pockets a little and take the chance that they may be among the few who will win the "Big One."

At most gaming tables along the Strip, action is fast and furious, with generally inflexible house rules. Downtown casinos are a bit more flexible when it comes to house rules, offering lower minimums and higher (sometimes no) limits. This attracts the unlikely combination of serious career gamblers and novices without much to spend. Still, the atmosphere is generally more relaxed and amiable, probably due to the fact that Downtown is a concentrated area similar to a small town—one that has not changed much in 70 years.

It is important to keep in mind that before you venture into any live gaming area, you should familiarize yourself with the basics of the games you intend to play. Despite the exceptions pointed out above, most experienced gamblers have little patience for the novice, as they see them as a bad omen in the

Calendar of Events

January *The Super Bowl:* The biggest sports betting day of the year; sports books are packed with anxious betters watching the game on giant screen televisions.

PBA Classic: A major stop on the Pro Bowlers tour, taking place at the Showboat every year.

February *Las Vegas International Marathon:* Really only a half marathon, but who could pass up the opportunity to run from Jean, Nevada, to the Strip on the old LA Highway?

April *World Series of Poker:* Twenty-one tournaments and prize money in the millions make this the biggest draw in the card world, attracting top players and crowds of spectators to Binion's Horseshoe in Downtown Las Vegas.

June *Helldorado Days:* A four-day rodeo and affiliated parties and pageants celebrate Southern Nevada's cowpoke roots.

September *Las Vegas 500K IRL race and NASCAR Craftsman Truck Series:* In what should be one of the biggest weekend racing combinations ever, these two races will be staged the same weekend at the end of September starting in 1999.

October *PGA Las Vegas Invitational:* A four-day, nationally televised golf tournament from the Tournament Players Club in Summerlin.

November *COMDEX:* The consumer-electronics industry descends on Las Vegas, meaning the streets are packed with traffic, hotel rooms are booked, and topless bars are crammed with revelers waving $1 bills.

December *CineVegas:* The premiere four-day film festival in Las Vegas, featuring a strong showing of premiere films, festival winners, and classics.

New Year's Eve: Celebrate with 200,000 of your newest friends. Las Vegas's celebrations and the two major block parties that accompany them are challenging Times Square for attendees. Make your reservations very early.

already frustrating situation of having to beat odds that are set against them. Also, there are strict rules as to what the player can do with his cards and chips, and where he can place his hands. Not knowing these rules can cost you a bet on the low end; repeated violations can lead to expulsion from the casino.

If you are completely inexperienced, there are several ways to overcome your lack of knowledge. The first would be to read about the games. Below is a very brief guide to the most popular games, while many books are sold locally that go to great lengths to explain each game.

Another method would be to practice on the electronic video version of the games before moving to the live tables. With minimum wagers as low as 5¢ and a distinct lack of potentially impatient players waiting for you to decide your next move, electronic gaming is an alternative that many novice gamblers never move beyond. Most casinos offer a variety of video game slot machines. Try Bally's for the latest selection; after all, they manufacture them.

> **More than 30 million annual visitors leave behind $6 billion of their hard-earned money at Las Vegas casinos.**

Despite the potentially intimidating aspects of live gaming, it makes little sense to spend your vacation in Las Vegas and not play at least a few hands of blackjack or craps, especially when there are free gaming lessons offered nearly everywhere. Gambling lessons are taught by dealers to groups of novices, so no one feels pressured or out of place. This hands-on method is the best way to learn a game and its rules without risking your money or your pride.

Baccarat

Typically assumed to be a high-roller card game, baccarat (bah-cah-rah) is similar to blackjack, though it's played with stricter rules, higher limits, and less player interaction. The object of the game is to come as close as possible to 9; the only real skill involved is deciding whether to bet on the player or the bank (i.e., the dealer). Most baccarat tables are located in quiet, sequestered sections of the casino. Gambling lessons are highly recommended for this game.

Big 6 (or Money Wheel)

This spin-and-win (or more often lose) game looks strangely like the prize games offered in carnivals of old. Its ease of learning—simply bet on one of the numbered wheel slots—attracts novices, but the house edge makes them walk away very quickly.

Bingo

Nearly everyone knows the game of bingo, the mini-lottery in which players try to line up a horizontal or vertical row of randomly drawn numbers. The numbers are drawn until

Most dealers are very friendly—just bone up on the rules of the game before you slide up to the table.

someone wins, and some veterans get up to 10 cards playing at once. No lessons are required.

Black Jack (or 21)

This is the most popular live table game played in Las Vegas—and the easiest card game to learn—owing to its relative simplicity. The object is to play against the dealer (house) to get as close to 21 as possible without "busting" (going over 21). There are several optional bets—splitting, doubling down, insurance—and variations that include single-deck vs. multi-deck card shoes and hands dealt face-up (as opposed to one card down). The house advantage is that if you bust, the dealer takes your money even if he busts as well.

Craps

This is the fabled game of cheering (and cursing) crowds, where everyone at the table has a stake in what one hapless gambler does with the dice. Loud players, dramatically placed chips, and flying dice all revolve around a set of complex betting rules and the fact that seven is more likely to be rolled than any other number. Money quickly changes hands at the craps table, making it another good candidate for lessons. Don't even lean against a busy craps table unless you know what you're doing and have plenty of money to lose.

Keno

Another game very similar to a lottery, keno is usually played while sitting in a hotel coffee shop. Unlike bingo, however, the odds are shifted in that players circle random numbers on a purchased ticket and wait for a fixed set of numbers to be drawn. It's easy to play: pick up to 15 numbers on the 80-number slip, then hand it and your money (usually a dollar per game) to the keno runner, and she'll return a computerized ticket. Watch the illuminated keno board above you to see if enough of your numbers come up to win. The odds of winning are very low—in fact, the house advantage is greater than that of any other casino game—but it's an inexpensive way to pass the time while you're dining.

Poker

A high-stakes card game played in a high-pressure atmosphere. Unlike most other card games, gamblers here play against each other; the house merely operates the game for a fixed percentage of the bets. There are many variations offered, from the standard 7-card stud to Texas Hold 'Em. This is another game in which lessons and lots of spare money are recommended. (As the old saying goes, "If you can't figure out who the fool is at the poker table, it's probably you.")

Pai Gow

If you enjoy poker, playing at mild pace, and playing against no house advantage, you'll love Pai Gow. Each player is dealt seven cards, which are then arranged by the player into two piles: one five-card hand and one two-card hand. Standard poker rules apply; that is, pairs, straights, flushes, full houses, etc. are ranked in a hierarchy of hands to determine the winner. The five card hand must beat the two card hand, and both hands must beat the dealer's two hands in order to win. If only one of the dealer's hands wins, the game is a "push" (tie), and no money changes hands (this happens more often than not). If both the dealer's hands win, you lose. It's also perfectly acceptable to ask the dealer for advice on how to play your hand (and a great way to learn). The caveat is that since the

> High rollers who bet as much as $100,000 on a single hand are known as "whales."

house has no advantage, it takes 5% of your winnings.

Roulette

Another subdued game of European fame, roulette does not enjoy much popularity in Las Vegas. It's a relatively simple game, where bets are placed by laying chips on a single number or groups of numbers, colors, or odd/even. Different players are given different colored chips to avoid confusion. The wheel is spun, the ball drops, and where it lands determines the outcome. Odds are as high as 35 to 1, which means a single $5 chip on the right number wins you $175. (Hint: avoid playing a double-zero wheel and search for those with only one zero.) Winning numbers are illuminated at each table to attract passers-by into thinking "It's hitting my number!"

Just pay and pull: simple slot machines are the most popular way to gamble.

Slots

Since the late 1970s, slot machines have become the most popular form of gaming in Las Vegas—so much so that they supersede the play at table games in many casinos. Though all modern slot machines are computerized, the rules are still the same: get three or four matching icons in a row (or some combination thereof) and you win. The difference is that the computer decides when you win, not pure chance. And even though the payback increases the more you bet on a single pull, the computer will decrease your odds of winning. The skill, they say, is to find a slot machine that's "hitting"; that is, a computer that's programmed to pay out big money. But what do you think the chances are of that happening very often?

Video Poker

Video poker has become increasingly popular, so much so that there's hardly a bar, grocery store, or laundromat in Las Vegas that doesn't have at least two or three machines. It's the same as regular five-card stud, with the machine acting as dealer. Unlike slots, interaction and a semblance of skill are required; that is, you are offered a choice on how to play the hand you're dealt. A chart on the screen lists the payoff of your winning hand and, as with slots, the more you bet, the better the payoff.

Weddings

Getting married almost ranks as a sport in Las Vegas, America's favorite city in which to tie the knot. More than 100,000 couples take the plunge here every year. Dozens of celebrities, including Michael Jordan, Elvis Presley, Paul Newman, and Richard Gere, have exchanged vows in Vegas; many of the chapels on Las Vegas Boulevard and Main Street have signs boasting of the big names they've joined in holy matrimony. Most weddings are anything but traditional. You can have an Elvis impersonator sing your nuptials at the Graceland Wedding Chapel (Tel. 702/ 474-6655), use the drive-up wedding window at Chapel by the Courthouse (Tel. 702/384-9099), or, if you're up to it, get married in a helicopter over the Strip. Other options range from a bungee-jumping ceremony to saying your vows on a boat on Lake Mead. Theme weddings—in "Star Trek" suits, for instance—have also become popular.

Versions of video poker range from "Jacks or Better" (the standard game) to "Deuces Wild" and "Double Bonus," though the more wild cards involved the lower the payoff.

THE BIG SHOWS

Once, Las Vegas showrooms were filled with top entertainment—headliners, comedians, production shows, and dancing girls—that could be enjoyed at a very low price. In that bygone era, elaborate dinner shows were considered a loss leader, a way to keep customers happily dropping money at the tables or the slot machines. As long as the bottom line shined, casino operators, especially those in the mob era, were happy to continue providing low-cost or even free entertainment and food.

The Little White Chapel is just one of the many places to get married in Las Vegas.

When corporations moved in with more stringent departmental accounting procedures, every sector of a hotel-casino had to show success. Not satisfied with a simple overall profit, corporate operators began to both raise prices and cut corners, resulting in an era of frustrating mediocrity from which Las Vegas has only recently emerged.

Most showrooms are again offering quality stars and elaborate productions, *sans* the accompanying dinner service. The prices have certainly risen, but so has the benchmark of quality. Some of the bigger shows and headliner appearances (especially during major events like New Year's Eve) exceed $100 per ticket—typical for New York City, but previously unheard of in Las Vegas. What this means is that, in the case of showroom entertainers, the old adage of getting what you pay for now applies equally to Las Vegas.

Although the runs for the shows listed here are considered open-ended, remember that nothing is static in Las Vegas. Entire resorts open and close, and showrooms sometimes change show times, prices, or entire featured productions. Also, there are numerous headlining entertainers that change from week to week. For current listings of all resort entertainment, pick up a free copy of *Showbiz Weekly* or *What's On In Las Vegas,* the two most comprehensive visitor guides. Below, "dark" refers to the day when the show does not play at all. Be advised that it is traditional for showgirls in Las Vegas production shows to be topless, and that tradition continues; many shows are not appropriate for children.

American Superstars: Of the cavalcade of impersonator shows, this one is skewed heavily toward the modern era. Talented performers provide energetic renditions of Madonna, Michael Jackson, Gloria Estefan, and Charlie Daniels, among others. And, yes, the Spice Girls impersonators still have Ginger. *Stratosphere Hotel and Casino, 2000 Las Vegas Boulevard South; Tel. (702) 380-7777. Shows 7 and 10pm, no late show Sunday–Tuesday; dark Thursday; $38 or less (special rate for children 4–12).*

Caesars Magical Empire: A particularly unusual interactive dinner and show experience set in a series of elaborately themed underground chambers rather than a showroom proper. Entertainers and illusionists perform while diners eat various courses and then move to another chamber. Fun for adults and children. *Cae-*

sars Palace Hotel and Casino, 3570 Las Vegas Boulevard South; Tel. (702) 731-7110. Multiple seatings start at 5pm; dark Sunday and Monday; around $75 (special rate for children 5–10).

Cirque du Soleil's Mystère: The internationally famed Cirque takes the circus to new levels of sophistication in an amazing state-of-the art theater. No animals are used in this circus, just 72 performers of amazing physical and emotive skill and grace. A most unique Las Vegas experience that borders on performance art. This popular show spawned the aquatic show at the Bellagio. *Treasure Island, 3300 Las Vegas Boulevard South; Tel. (702) 894-7111. Shows 7:30 and 10:30pm; dark Monday and Tuesday; over $60.*

Cirque du Soleil's O: The latest from the acclaimed international troupe, O dazzles in an aquatic environment that utilizes 1½ million gallons (6.8 million liters) of water. True to the Cirque tradition, there are no animals, just 75

Cirque du Soleil's Mystère, a circus without animals but with a whole lot of style.

skilled performers. *Bellagio Hotel and Casino, 3600 Las Vegas Boulevard South; Tel. (702) 693-7111. Shows 7:30 and 11pm; dark Wednesday and Thursday; over $100.*

Danny Gans – The Man of Many Voices: What started as a short-lived Las Vegas stint at the Stratosphere Tower has evolved into one of the most popular shows in Las Vegas. Gans is an amazing impersonator and an energetic showman who has mastered the art of entertainment. *Mirage Hotel and Casino, 7900 Las Vegas Boulevard South; Tel. (702) 791-7111. Shows 8pm; dark Monday and Friday; over $60.*

EFX: A grand $45 million production show in a classic but updated style. Featuring a host of original music sung by the main star (at writing, Tommy Tune) and dozens of other singing and dancing talents, EFX is a special-effects laden science-fiction tale suitable for all ages. *MGM Grand Hotel and Casino, 3799 Las Vegas Boulevard South; Tel. (702) 891-7777. Shows 7:30 and 10:30pm; dark Sunday and Monday; over $50.*

Wayne Newton: Las Vegas's copnsummate entertainer, Wayne Newton croons to audiences six nights a week in an elaborate new theater named for "Mr. Vegas" himself. *Stardust Resort and Casino, 3000 Las Vegas Boulevard South; Tel. (702) 732-6111. Shows 9pm Sunday–Thursday; 8 and 11pm Saturday; dark Friday; $60 or less.*

Blue Man Group: This award-winning (albeit unusual) show features three bald, blue characters. The one-of-a-kind showroom experience has been called innovative, hilarious, and musically powerful. *Luxor Hotel and Casino, 3900 Las Vegas Boulevard South; Tel. (702) 262-4100. Shows 7 and 10pm (no late show Sunday and Monday); dark Tuesday; over $50.*

Jubilee!: Long before the blockbuster movie, Jubilee! was sinking the Titanic on the Strip in what is the show's

Whether part of a show or just the decor, there's spectacle everywhere: here, Cleopatra's Barge at Caesars Palace.

signature amazing special effect. The show also features magician Dirk Arthur and dozens of topless and costumed showgirls, making this an event for adults only. *Bally's Hotel and Casino, 3645 Las Vegas Boulevard South; Tel. (702) 967-4111. Shows 7:30 and 10:30pm Wednesday–Monday; dark Tuesday; $45–60.*

King Arthur's Tournament: A radical departure from modern Las Vegas stage shows, this one features two unusual elements: live horses and dinner—the latter of which is eaten without utensils. A re-creation of a medieval knights' jousting tournament, it's great fun for families. *Excalibur Hotel and Casino, 3850 Las Vegas Boulevard South; Tel. (702) 597-7777. Shows 6 and 8:30pm; $45 or less.*

Legends In Concert: The favorite of many return visitors, this classic Las Vegas impersonation show features all the greats from yesterday and today. Impersonators render

*Siegfried and Roy are a
Las Vegas fixture—
literally and figuratively.*

uncanny performances of the Four Tops and Elvis, as well as modern stars like Michael Jackson and Tina Turner. *Imperial Palace Hotel and Casino, 3535 Las Vegas Boulevard South; Tel. (702) 731-3311. Shows 7:30 and 10:30pm; dark Sunday; $35 or less.*

Master Magician Lance Burton: Set in perhaps the most magnificent environment in Las Vegas—an impeccably gilded theater that somehow maintains intimacy—magician Lance Burton pulls off extraordinary illusions with the assistance of a talented group of dancers. *Monte Carlo Hotel and Casino, 3770 Las Vegas Boulevard South; Tel. (702) 730-7777. Shows 7 and 10pm; dark Sunday and Monday; $60 or less.*

Michael Flatley's Lord of the Dance: From the heralded choreographer of Riverdance comes this Las Vegas production, an internationally recognized hit featuring over 40 talented dancers in an amazing show of traditional and modern dance. *New York-New York Hotel and Casino, 3790 Las Vegas Boulevard South; Tel. (702) 740-6969. Shows 7:30 and 10:30pm Tuesday, Wednesday, Saturday; 9pm Thursday and Friday; dark Sunday and Monday; $50–80.*

Siegfried and Roy: These world-famous illusionists and Las Vegas residents have risen from a small-time specialty act to stardom. Their famous white tigers are an integral part of the show, set in a 1500-seat showroom. *Mirage Hotel and Casino, 3400 Las Vegas Boulevard South; Tel. (702) 791-7444. Shows 7:30 and 11pm; dark Wednesday and Thursday; over $60.*

Splash: One of the few remaining "traditional" Vegas production shows, Splash features a large cast of singers and dancers who perform around variety acts. There are numerous set and theme changes, plenty of water use, and a number in which the dancers (topless at the late show) come into the audience. *Riviera Hotel and Casino, 2901 Las Vegas Boulevard South; Tel. (702) 734-5110. Shows 7:30 and 10:30pm; $36–60.*

The Best of the Folies Bergères…Sexier Than Ever: The home of the topless dancers of the Folies Bergères since 1961, the Tropicana's show was recently revamped and updated. Nothing says "Las Vegas" quite like this; the glittering costumes and chorus line of showgirls is what the myth was based on. *Tropicana Resort and Casino, 3801 Las Vegas Boulevard South; Tel. (702) 739-2222. Shows 7:30 and 10pm; dark Thursday; $40–60.*

SHOPPING

Where there is money, there is shopping—or so it should seem. As with everything else in Las Vegas, shopping facilities have always been around, but when compared with other major cities, they did not live up to expectation. Hotel shopping areas consisted of retailers selling primarily expensive and tacky (or sometimes cheap and tacky) merchandise, and malls were utilitarian outlets of typical retail stores. This scenario has changed dramatically in recent years.

As the city expands, so do the shopping facilities. Upscale department stores have arrived at suburban malls in recent years, challenging the stalwarts like Sears and Dillard's. Additionally, top name designers now have retail locations in several hotel shopping facilities. The development of new malls such as the Forum Shops (at Caesars Palace) has in some cases single-handedly elevated the state of shopping in the city, with even more major hotel-based shopping promenades having emerged at the recently opened Aladdin and Venetian resorts.

As if the explosion of retail shopping malls was not enough to quell the demand, there are outlet malls in abundance within a short drive, and a handful of local shops that deserve attention.

Retail Shopping Malls

The Forum Shops at Caesars (Tel. 702/893-4800), a themed indoor shopping promenade built to look and feel

The Forum Shops at Caesars offer an upscale shopping experience enjoyed by visitors and locals alike.

like an outdoor Roman street, surprised quite a few observers in 1992 by attracting not only the obvious tourists from the Strip, but also more than a handful of shopping-starved locals eager to explore stores they once had to travel out of state to visit. A 1997 expansion then doubled the space. From DKNY to FAO Schwarz, dozens of top retailers have their only Las Vegas location here. The number of excellent restaurants and entertainment outlets makes this a great place for an all-day, one-stop spending spree.

Also on the Strip, **The Fashion Show Mall** (Tel. 702/369-8382) was for years the only high-fashion shopping source for tourists and residents with excess cash. Though it has since been eclipsed by the Forum Shops, many big name department stores absent from the Forum and other area malls are located here (Saks Fifth Avenue and Neiman Marcus among them). A generous selection of restaurants, from fast food to fabulous, satiate the hunger brought on by walking the mall's long wings.

Stepping away from the Strip, the **Boulevard Mall** (Tel. 702/732-8949) was the first of its type in Las Vegas. As with many places in the city, it was recently remodeled and expanded, making it again one of the city's most popular stops for standard mall shopping. Its proximity to the Strip make it popular for tourists as well.

The Galleria at Sunset (Tel. 702/434-0202) is the most recent of the suburban shopping malls. Located in the upscale Green Valley area of Henderson, across from the Sunset Station Hotel and Casino, the mall houses interesting specialty stores in addition to department stores, as well as a huge food court.

Despite a recent renovation, the **Meadows Mall** (Tel. 702/878-4849) is the least appealing of the three suburban malls. At one point the crown jewel of Las Vegas shopping, the mall now resides in a central and older region of the valley, sandwiched between middle-class families and uppercrust long-timers. While the shopping selection is similar to the other suburban malls, sadly, the atmosphere is not.

Factory Outlet Malls

The **Fashion Outlet Mall** (Tel. 702/874-1400) at Primm, Nevada (on the California state line) is the latest entry into the outlet mall roster, and the best. Though it requires a 30-minute drive from Tropicana via I-15 (or the free shuttle from New York-New York; Tel. 1-888-424-6898), the Fashion Outlet's selection of top names (Guess, Kenneth Cole, Tommy Hilfiger) and specialty stores (such as Williams Sonoma) make it worth the effort.

Within the valley is the **Belz Factory Outlet World** (Tel. 702/896-5599). Belz, an indoor mall, offers 145 stores ranging from clothing to electronics.

Selected Local Shopping

Beyond the malls lie hundreds of unique specialty stores. From ethnic food shops and vintage clothing stores to electronics and book shops, there are so many interesting shopping spots that it is hard to imagine their breadth and depth. The following are a few Las Vegas highlights; for a more thorough listing of specialty stores, pick up one of the free alternative newsweeklies, *CityLife* or *Las Vegas Weekly*.

The Attic (Tel. 702/388-4088) is perhaps the most famous vintage store in America, owing to its feature in both a Visa commercial and on extreme sports network ESPN II. A massive two-story collection of vintage clothes, appliances and knick-knacks, the Attic serves an international audience with its wide selection of period clothing. They are often called upon to provide items for movies being filmed in Las Vegas.

On the other end of the scale, the **Tower/WOW! Multimedia Superstore** (Tel. 702/364-2500) sells nothing even remotely vintage, except perhaps within its vast CD selection. A combined effort of Tower Records and the Good Guys Electronics, WOW! overwhelms in every way. To the right is a huge electronics and computer selection featuring a home theater room and a classical listening room. To the left are innumerable aisles of records, books, software, CDs, 12-inch vinyl, and the city's largest selection of periodicals and 'zines. At the fulcrum is a coffee bar and café under a giant screen television flanked by CD listening stations.

Those who wear glasses will appreciate the Strip location of **Optica of Las Vegas** (Tel. 702/735-8557), a full service optometry shop that can repair eyewear, provide exams, and set visitors up with a new set of prescription glasses or contact lenses—all within a day or two. The designer frame selection is among the best in town.

True to its all-inclusive mentality, Las Vegas offers good shopping and good dining—often side-by-side.

Three pro courses and perennially excellent weather make Las Vegas the perfect place to hit the green.

For souvenirs of the innately Las Vegas kind, there is the **Gamblers' General Store** (Tel. 702/382-9903), a centrally located supplier of slot machines, gaming tables, and other gaming accoutrements. Most items can be shipped for the purchaser by request.

For a taste of authentic Indian tobacco, the **Paiute Tribal Smoke Shop** (Tel. 702/387-6433) sells tax-free tobacco products through its drive-through window, so you can cruise right back to the hotel and spend all that money you just saved.

SPORTS

Las Vegas is a sporting city. Whether you want to watch championship boxing matches, bet on the New York Giants at a sports book, or play 18 holes of golf, all it takes is the right toys and/or plenty of cash. If you engage in outdoor sports, remember that valley temperatures can reach well above 100° F (38° C) in summer and below freezing in winter after the sun drops below the mountains. Take all necessary precautions when participating in any outdoor sport.

Spectator Sports

Boxing

Las Vegas has a rich boxing history, having hosted enough championship matches to qualify as a capital of the sport. A big-time bout at one of the three resorts that handle most of the action—the MGM Grand (Tel. 702/891-7777), Caesars Palace (Tel. 702/731-7110), or The Mirage (Tel. 702/791-7111)—invariably draws a crowd heavy with celebrities.

The National Finals Rodeo

Held every December, this is one of the largest—and richest—rodeo events in the country, featuring 10 days of the nation's top cowboys and cowgirls riding bulls, busting broncos, and roping calves at the Thomas and Mack Center. The city goes western with endless satellite events: beauty pageants, parties and dances at bars, cowboy-themed art exhibits, musical events at Downtown's Fremont Street Experience, and golf tournaments. If you wish to attend, plan ahead—last-minute tickets to the big rodeo events are hard to come by.

Motor Sports

Serious auto racing arrived in Las Vegas in 1996 with the opening of the Las Vegas Motor Speedway, 17 miles (27 km) north of Downtown on Interstate 15. The 1,500-acre (607-hectare) site is a speed-freak's dream: a 1½-mile (2½-

km) tri-oval super speedway, smaller clay and paved ovals, a drag strip, a road track, and a motocross course. Race fans fill the 107,000-seat facility for NASCAR events like the Las Vegas 300, Winston West, and Craftsman Truck races, as well as the IRL Las Vegas 500.

Golf Tournaments

The Las Vegas Invitational held every fall—famed as Tiger Woods' first professional tournament in 1996—is considered the city's top golf attraction. Three courses split the action: the TPC at the Canyons, Southern Highlands, and the main course, the TPC at Summerlin. The TPC at the Canyons is home to the Las Vegas Senior Classic, a top draw for golf's big names held every spring. Check the PGA website at <www.pgatour.com> for complete information on tournaments and on other golf events.

Bowling

Las Vegas has always had an affinity for bowling. The PBA holds both national and senior televised tournaments here at the Showboat Bowling Center in January.

Other Sports

Las Vegas, while lacking a major sports franchise, is home to a triple-A baseball team and a minor-league hockey squad. The Las Vegas Stars—the city's longest-running professional sports outfit—is a farm team for baseball's San Diego Padres; tickets are usually available for the Cashman Field home games. The Las Vegas Thunder hockey team (which is not affiliated with any NHL franchise) competes in the Thomas and Mack Center. During football and basketball seasons, the University of Nevada, Las Vegas fields teams in both sports. UNLV's basketball team has a storied history, winning the NCAA title in 1990.

Participatory Sports

Golf

For a desert city, Las Vegas has more than enough grass fairways and water hazards to keep the most avid duffer busy. For a locator map and a course-by-course description, go to <www.lasvegasfreedom.com>. The Rio Suites Hotel maintains a course several miles away from the Strip for their guests that offers spectacular views of the Las Vegas Valley. Angel Park Golf Club (Tel. 702/254-4653) is a municipal course with a difference: it has two 18-hole courses designed by Arnold Palmer and a 12-hole par-3 course featuring replicas of famous par-3 holes from around the world. The Las Vegas Paiute Resort (Tel. 702/658-1400) is 20 miles (32 km) north of town but worth the mileage: One of its two courses—called Snow Mountain—was designated the best public course in Southern Nevada by *Golf Digest*. Also beyond city limits is the Legacy Golf Club (Tel. 702/897-2200) in the nearby suburb of Henderson.

Rock Climbing

Red Rock Canyon (Tel. 702/363-1921), just 20 minutes from the Strip, boasts some of the best rock climbing in the western United States. There are literally thousands of climbing challenges, from small bouldering routes to towering, experts-only cliffs. Spring and fall are optimum climbing seasons, but almost any weekend will find a cross-section of the international rock-jock community roping up in the canyon. Sky's the Limit guide service (Tel. 702/363-4533) can arrange climbing trips of nearly any duration. For a more climate-controlled climb, try the indoor climbing mountain at Game-Works on the Strip (see page 100). At 75 ft (23 m) it is said to be among the world's highest.

Hiking

The Las Vegas Valley is rimmed with quality hiking trails. One of the more scenic is the five-mile River Mountain Trail (Tel. 702/293-2034), which offers fine views of both Lake Mead and the Las Vegas Valley. Red Rock Canyon affords numerous routes, including a two-mile Pine Creek Canyon trek and a slightly longer walk along the Keystone Thrust Trail. Likewise, Mount Charleston is webbed with many good hikes; the ranger station there can supply more information (702/873-8800). Valley of Fire (see page 66) is also a popular hiking spot.

Bicycling

Avoid putting your mettle to the peddle on the city's busier streets; bike paths are few and courteous drivers even fewer. The best places are local parks or bike-friendly spots beyond city limits. One favorite: the 13-mile (21-km) scenic loop at Red Rock Canyon (see page 67), takes cyclists through some of the area's more picturesque landscapes and is not overly taxing.

Mountain bikers can call Escape the City Streets (Tel. 702/596-2953) to arrange a more rugged ride through the canyon's Cottonwood Valley. Another good bet: Floyd Lamb State Park (702/486-5413), a few miles north on US 95. The bike paths wind among ponds, trees, and historic buildings.

Tennis

Most resorts have tennis facilities for guests only. Otherwise, the Las Vegas Sporting House (Tel. 702/733-8999), a membership sporting club, makes its courts available to nonmembers as well, and several additional courts can be found in Lorenzi Park.

Snow Sports

Mount Charleston has a ski area, the Las Vegas Ski and Snowboard Resort, also known as Lee Canyon (Tel. 702/872-5462). It has bunny, intermediate, and expert routes, along with all the trappings: ski rental, ski school, and a lounge. The natural snowfall is often augmented by snow-making equipment to ensure adequate powder. The Las Vegas Ski and Snowboard Resort has nine long runs on 40 acres (16 hectares); despite its name, snowboarding is allowed only at certain times.

ADULT ENTERTAINMENT

For all the hype about Las Vegas's conversion to a family town, the unrelenting truth is that beyond all the shiny new big name properties lies a bevy of adult-oriented distractions. While in the recent past efforts were made to eliminate many of these attractions, the actual result was that most of the more seedy or disreputable businesses have disappeared while those operating within the law have flourished. Las Vegas now seems poised to accept the multiple layers of its existence as a tourist city.

Most of the resorts on the Strip have appeased family visitors by cleaning up their shows and covering up the showgirls. But at the **Riviera** (Tel. 702/734-5110) all four

Smoke and mirrors: here, the Rio Casino's show.

shows are adult-oriented (though Splash is covered for the early show); for raucous fun, choose the "Crazy Girls"—a topless review that gets even more red-light during convention season.

There are also dozens of clubs that offer either nude or topless entertainment. Of the topless-only clubs (all of which have full bars), the two best are **Cheetah's Topless Lounge**, 2112 Western Avenue (Tel. 702/384-0074), an intimate, friendly place, and **Olympic Garden Cabaret**, 1531 Las Vegas Boulevard South (Tel. 702/385-8987) which, with eleven full-size stages, is quite the opposite. For totally nude dancers, the choices are just as varied, but only one—the venerable **Palomino Club**, 1848 Las Vegas Boulevard North (Tel. 702/642-2984)—serves alcohol. Of the numerous others that do not, the best bet is the tastefully decorated but oddly named **Spearmint Rhino**, 3340 S. Highland Drive; Tel. (702) 796-3600.

Las Vegas shines when the sun sets: the Strip as seen looking north from Bellagio.

NIGHTLIFE

For all there is to do and see in Las Vegas, one may wonder if there is a nightlife at all outside of the obvious. The answer is a resounding yes. From local bars featuring live music and comedy, to nightclubs, cafés and coffeehouses, the city's nightlife beyond gambling and shows is very healthy. For a detailed listing of local events beyond the Strip, pick up one of the two free alternative newsweeklies, *CityLife* or *Las Vegas Weekly*.

Nightclubbing has come of age in Las Vegas, thanks to a resurgence of dance music and the city's population boom. **Club Utopia** (Tel. 702/390-4650), on the Strip but not in a hotel, may be single-handedly responsible for reviving the dying Las Vegas nightclub scene by taking the metropolitan sounds of techno and house out of the underground and into a commercial Las Vegas venue for the first time. That, along with the success of **Club Rio** (Tel. 702/252-7727) in the Rio Suites Hotel, led to a deluge of new hotel-based high energy clubs, including **Ra** in the Luxor (Tel. 702/262-4000), **Studio 54** in the MGM Grand (Tel. 702/891-1111), and more scheduled to open soon. Each caters to a specific crowd, so hunt around until you find the one right for you.

Other nightclubs place as much emphasis on drinking as dancing, including **Drink Las Vegas** (Tel. 702/796-5519), a fabulous two-story nightclub with numerous bars serving every drink known to man. **The Beach** (Tel. 702/731-1925) is also two stories high, with waiters and waitresses dressed for sunbathing—they often jump on the bar for a little bikini dancing.

Lesbian and gay travelers will find integrated nightlife in the so-called "Gay Triangle" area on Paradise Road. **Gipsy** (Tel. 702/731-1919) is small but wall-to-wall with energetic dancing (it's mostly men here, though women are welcome). Across the street, **Lace** (Tel. 702/791-0100) is a tiny women's disco in the back of Angles video bar.

The café scene is surprisingly strong for a city with so many Starbucks outlets. **Café Copioh** (Tel. 702/739-0305) is a well known haunt of university students and professors, and hosts a calendar of events ranging from poetry readings to live music. Nearby is the venerable **Café Espresso Roma** (Tel. 702/369-1540)—the oldest coffeehouse in Las Vegas and, according to some, still the best in all its Bohemian glory.

For less caffeine and more food, across town in the Downtown Gateway District is the egalitarian **Enigma Garden Café** (Tel. 702/386-0999). Lawyers, poets, city councilmen, and starving musicians partake day and night of its garden setting and large menu featuring items with names of historic Las Vegas importance. In the opposite direction you'll enjoy **Jazzed Cafe and Vinoteca** (Tel. 702/798-5995), a charming bistro with a magnificent by-the-glass wine list and a carefully crafted menu of Tuscan specialties accompanied by acid jazz, tiramisù and espresso. Best of all, it's open until about 4am.

LAS VEGAS FOR CHILDREN

Although Las Vegas is better known as an adult town, there are a surprising number of kid-friendly activities. Most casinos have at least some kind of arcade, but the true high-scorer is **GameWorks** (Tel. 702/895-7626), next to the MGM Grand, with 47,000 sq ft (4371 sq m) of games (more than 250) from traditional pin-ball outposts to high-tech diversions. If you play up an appetite, GameWorks also has a full-service restaurant, snack bar, and Starbucks Coffee outlet. Adults may relax in the bar and shoot pool while the kiddies shoot each other.

Add a little zoom to your kids' day with a stop at **Sahara Speedworld** (Tel. 702/737-2111), a huge (40,000-sq-ft /3720-sq-m) playground of virtual reality auto racing in life-size race cars, dozens of interactive rides, and two 3-D theaters.

The Big Shot offers a big thrill and a big view of Las Vegas 1,100 feet (335 meters) below.

Visitors between May and September can take tots and teens alike for a cool dip at the **Wet 'N Wild** water park (Tel. 702/737-3819). There are kiddie pools and knee-buckling water slides. Der Stuka offers a seven-story drop, while the Black Hole shoots you through a dark tunnel. Or just float along in the slow-moving lazy river or drift in the large wave pool.

In recent years, as it sought to attract more families, Las Vegas has become a city of theme parks. The MGM is a grand example. At the **MGM Grand Adventure Theme Park** (Tel. 702/891-7777; open spring and summer only), visitors can raft a small river, take a 200-ft (61-m) freefall from the Sky Screamer, watch a colorful sea battle, or chat with strolling MGM characters.

Decades ago, Circus Circus inaugurated the era of family friendly hotel-casino, and in recent years has tried to up the ante with **Grand Slam Canyon** (Tel. 702/734-0410), a pink-dome-covered, climate-controlled cluster of attractions: the

Kids get a kick out of the "rain forest," complete with a jungle pool, inside the Mirage Hotel.

Canyon Blaster corkscrew roller coaster, a water ride, bumper cars, carnival games, and a laser tag arena. It's located behind the venerable hotel-casino, which itself features kid-friendly free circus acts from 11am to midnight daily.

Roller coaster aficionados will want to hop aboard the twisting, turning, looping **Manhattan Express roller coaster** at New York-New York. While inside, stop at the extensive Coney Island-themed arcade. Equal thrills can be had atop the **Stratosphere Tower**, where you will find a slingshot ride called the **Big Shot**. Its sudden vertical acceleration is accentuated by its setting 1,100 ft (335 m) above the city. There is a roller coaster up there as well, but experienced riders consider it too slow and uneventful despite the altitude.

Next to the MGM Grand you will find **M&M World**, four stories of merchandise and memorabilia dedicated to the candy that doesn't melt in your hand. Inside is an

8,500-sq-ft (791-sq-m) store loaded with thousands of M&M knickknacks.

Want to get the kids away from the casinos? Try the three-course miniature golf, bumper boats, go-carts and arcade games at **Scandia Family Fun Center** (Tel. 702/364-0070).

Even farther from the lights is **Bonnie Springs-Old Nevada** (Tel. 702/875-4191), a mock ghost town near Red Rock Canyon. The wild-West town comes complete with gunfights, a wax museum, an opera house, a mini-train, horseback riding, and an extensive petting zoo.

For motorized thrills, Las Vegas has at least one grand prix go-cart course. **Las Vegas Mini Gran Prix** (Tel. 702/259-7000) boasts the west's only banked-oval stock car track. Parents, bring your driving gloves—along with go-carts and kiddie carts, the 7-acre (3-hectare) facility has wheels for adults as well.

For something a little more aggressive, **Desert Storm Paintball** (702/595-2555) puts paintball guns in the hands of budding warriors—over age 10, that is.

LOCAL ARTS

Although Las Vegas isn't known for its culture, that doesn't mean it hasn't any. Anchor tenants in the local arts scene include the long-lived **Nevada Ballet Theatre** (Tel. 702/243-2623), which has toured the country and the world with its original productions. The visual and performing arts departments of the **University of Nevada, Las Vegas** also constitute a center of cultural activity. The **Summerlin Library and Performing Arts Center** (Tel. 702/256-5111) features an art gallery (as do most library branches in the area) and frequent music and theater performances. Activity information is available through the **Nevada Arts Council** (Tel. 702/486-3700).

EATING OUT

The Myth: Visitors to Las Vegas often expect to find a dining paradise offering excellent around-the-clock meals at abnormally low prices. As the story goes, casino dining rooms surround guests with opulence, attentive service, and only the best food served over tables draped in white linen; buffets are heaped with delicious, never-ending food offered for a flat rate lower than the cost of an average fast food meal. Gamblers are rewarded for their play by pit bosses generously scribbling out "comps" (complimentary tickets) for the hotel's on-site restaurants. The level of the comp depends upon the level of play, so everyone—low rollers to big spenders—can be accommodated. Nothing could be better than a free meal in Las Vegas.

The Truth: Until recently, the quality of dining in Las Vegas was, overall, unexceptional and pedestrian. Hotel-casinos, which

were once the only places visitors and locals could go to dine out, offered a standard selection of options that were based more on price than palate: one 24-hour coffee shop, one buffet, one middle-of-the road ethnic dining room, and one pricey "gourmet room" offering steaks, seafood, and little else.

Beyond the Strip and Downtown, the dining story

Steven Spielberg's "Dive!" has many delicious choices perfect to dive in to.

Wining and dining in Las Vegas have gone from passable to first-class in the last few years.

was even more dismal. With a few notable exceptions, choices were limited to low-end franchises and fast food.

The Solution: Thankfully, major strides have been made in Las Vegas's dining options. With the arrival of Wolfgang Puck's Spago at the Forum Shops in 1992, the city began a slow but sure ascent from the depths of continental cuisine into the modern world of the nouvelle, haute, California, Pan Asian, and Pacific Rim. Since then, more recognizable chefs have infiltrated Las Vegas, among them Emeril Lagasse and Jean-Louis Palladin.

Acting in concert with these arrivals was the hotels' newfound willingness to relinquish ownership and management of some of their restaurant spaces to experienced restaurateurs. While this was responsible for an overall increase in prices, the result for food lovers has been wonderful. The improvement of the dining experience and the resulting rise of diners' expectations led to an across-the-board renewal. Today, some of the city's—even the West's—best restaurants are ensconced within hotels, such as the Rio's Napa and the Santa Fe's Suzette's.

Gimme Buffet

Despite this, the buffets are still a real hit-and-miss affair, with most of them offering similar selections of prime rib, starchy vegetables, limp salads, and boring desserts. They often offer a wide array of cuisines—Mexican, Italian, American heartland (that is, meat and potatoes), and vegetables—plus all the seconds, thirds, and fourths you can gulp down. The tantalizing buffets of lore—where the food is imaginatively selected and the prices low—do exist, but one has to search for them. The Feast at Palace Station is in this category, as is Main Street Station's Garden Court Buffet. The Rio's Carnival World Buffet is also very good and has an incredibly large selection, though it is often crowded and not priced low enough to qualify as a traditional bargain. The very best of the lot (the Golden Nugget's The Buffet, for example) are no longer cheap, while Bellagio's price has reached new heights.

Sunday Champagne Brunches were once the best of the buffets, despite champagne that was not always palatable. Today, most are simply a more expensive version of the standard breakfast-lunch offerings. Bally's Sterling Brunch is a notable exception. Replete with ice sculptures, and fresh flowers, it is a spread fit for a king; it is also the most expensive, at $50.

A Restaurant Revolution

Theme restaurants have proliferated in Las Vegas. Local versions of the Hard Rock Cafe, the Harley Davidson Café, and Planet Hollywood pull the same surprisingly brisk business as they do around the globe.

One of the traditional areas of any major tourist city—a so-called restaurant row—has evolved piecemeal along Paradise

Road, adding to the options. Here, diners can choose from a plethora of major restaurants, locally-owned eateries, and some small tasty ethnic cafés, all within a short distance of one another.

Outside the resort corridors, franchises have always played a big role. From fast food to pancake houses to low-price family diners, chains suck up much of the local dining budget. When the population skyrocketed in the mid 1990s, some of the better chains made their way to the valley; for a town starved of choice for so long, names like Bertolini's and P. F. Chang's sound heavenly.

The Hard Rock Cafe offers an American meal among music memorablilia.

Locally-owned dining is also experiencing a welcome increase in availability and quality, with numerous ethnic and specialty restaurants opening. From the laid back atmosphere of the Mediterranean Café (serving Middle Eastern specialties like falafel and hummous) to the homey environment of Chicago Joe's, and the artsy and elegant European vibe of Jazzed Café, the town's best medium-priced variety is often found outside the resort areas.

In fact, considering how rapidly the dining situation has improved—and the gobs of money big resorts are paying to lure world-class chefs—it probably won't be long before Las Vegas joins the culinary ranks of San Francisco and New York.

HANDY TRAVEL TIPS

An A–Z Summary of Practical Information

A

ACCOMMODATIONS (See also CAMPING, YOUTH HOSTELS, and the list of RECOMMENDED HOTELS starting on page 125)

Las Vegas is a unique city in that the vast majority of its hotels offer both accommodations and attractions. Most of the places travelers want to see are found along the Strip or Downtown, so staying in one of these areas will put you right in the center of the action.

The quality of accommodations can range from the best to very questionable, but most of the **hotel-casinos** fall into the comfortably average to above-average categories. Off-Strip hotel-casinos offer many of the same amenities—and sometimes more—as on-Strip hotels, and often at a lesser price. Neighborhood hotel-casinos usually offer less in the way of amenities, but make up for it in price.

There are **non-gaming resorts** (such as the Alexis Park) if you prefer classy accommodations away from the clang of slot machines. Also, there are **non-gaming motels** all over the city, in the suburbs, and along Boulder Highway. Many of them specialize in extended stays of a week or more, and can be very good alternatives for travelers on a budget.

If you will be without a car, be sure to choose a hotel as close to your preferred area of action as possible; Las Vegas is spread widely, taxis are costly, and the public transportation system, though making strides, is not yet up to speed.

As there is no truly slow season in Las Vegas, room reservations are strongly suggested, especially during heavy travel periods in the fall and spring and on any weekend, during any major sporting event, for New Year's Eve, and whenever there is a major trade convention in town. In fact, some of the conventions draw over 200,000 people (that's not a misprint)—enough to fill almost every room in the city. The **Las Vegas Convention and Visitors Authority** at (702) 892-0711 can alert you to when the events are in town, and will assist with room reservations and just about any other travel questions you may have. Travelers with internet access should also search **www.vegas.com**.

If you have trouble finding a vacancy, try calling **Reservations Plus** at 1-800-805-9528 (toll-free in the US). Not only can they find and book you a room in your price range (often at a discount), they can also arrange entertainment packages as well. Best of all, the service is free.

Las Vegas

Despite these warnings, there are periods of relative quiet when rates are down and it is easier to find a room without reservations. The city is usually slower between Thanksgiving (last Thursday of November) and Christmas, as well as during the heat of July and August.

AIRPORT

Las Vegas is served by one major airport, McCarran International (Tel. 702/261-5211). With the rapid growth in travel to Las Vegas, the airport is among the world's busiest, and recently added 26 gates to handle the flow. The airport is also located very close to town, within a 15-minute drive of Tropicana Avenue and the Strip. Transportation to and from the airport is available via an unending stream of taxis.

For a cheaper ride, try one of the shuttle buses that operate 24 hours and take you directly to your hotel for as little as $5. One such company is **Bell Trans** (Tel. 702/739-7990). There is also a public bus that serves the airport, but it takes significantly longer than the relatively inexpensive shuttle buses.

B

BICYCLE RENTAL/HIRE

Bicycle riding within the city is not advised. For bicycle tours of the surrounding natural areas, call **Escape the City Streets**; Tel. (702) 596-2953.

BUDGETING for YOUR TRIP

Gone are the days when hotels and food were to be had for next to nothing, though prices are still a bargain when compared to large cities like New York. Plan on spending the same in Las Vegas on most items as on a similarly elaborate trip to Los Angeles.

Setting and holding yourself to a budget, especially one for **gambling**, is an important part of any trip to Las Vegas. Decide before leaving home exactly how much per day you will budget for gambling and do not permit yourself to exceed that amount; access to bank accounts via ATM cards is far too easy, and many only dole out

$100s. More than a few travelers have arrived here seeking fortune and were forced to sell a prized possession for a return fare.

Tipping must be budgeted for as well. It is a recognized and accepted part of Las Vegas culture, and being unprepared can result in poor service (see TIPPING).

C

CAMPING

Within the city, there are plenty of RV parks to accommodate road travelers, as well as a **KOA** (Tel. 702/451-5527) on Boulder Highway that has both RV and the only in-town tent sites. On the Strip, Circus-Circus has a massive RV park, while many others exist beyond the Strip such as those at Sam's Town and the Showboat, both on Boulder Highway.

Outside of the city, camping is plentiful in the Red Rock Canyon, Lake Mead, Valley of Fire, and Mt. Charleston natural areas, with Red Rock being only 15 minutes from the city (see Excursions, page 63).

CAR RENTAL/HIRE

The low, thin spread of Las Vegas—over 20 times the physical size of San Francisco—makes travel by vehicle a requirement anytime one wants to go further than a few blocks beyond the Strip and Downtown. Taxis will make the trip but are rarely seen outside the resort areas, and the city's buses are reliable but slow and sometimes crowded.

Visitors who want any degree of freedom rent cars and most do so right at the airport upon arrival. As with accommodations, advance reservations are suggested but not as essential, though the same warnings apply. The local telephone directory lists 17 pages of rental agencies, with all of the major US companies being represented (Alamo, Avis, Budget, Dollar, Enterprise, Hertz, National, and Thrifty), and rates are usually below the US average in cost. The major companies usually will not rent to anyone under 25 years old, but some of the local companies will. All rental companies require a driver's license and most ask for a major credit card matching the license. Price quotes do not include taxes or liability and collision damage waivers (CDW). Adding these on can double the cost, so be sure to check with your credit card company to see what is already covered. No added insurance is required, but renters should carefully weigh their responsibility when making that choice, especially in an aggressive driving city such as Las Vegas.

CHILDREN

Children should not be left unattended in casino or hotel areas. Persons under the age of 21 are not permitted in any casino gaming areas, bars, or lounges for any reason. Most casinos are child-friendly if the rules are followed (children may walk through the casino when accompanied by a parent but may not stop), while others ban strollers from the premises or close the doors entirely to those under 18 unless they are guests staying with an adult. Most hotels offer babysitting services if necessary.

CLIMATE

Las Vegas is a desert region, making summer temperatures very warm and dry and winters cold. August temperatures can reach over 115° F (46° C) in the mid-afternoon, and still hover around 100 degrees at midnight. Winter temperatures can be surprisingly brisk, dipping very quickly after the sun sets. Spring is warmer but windy; fall is often the best time to visit, with warm days and mild nights. The sun shines an average of 305 days per year, so bring sunglasses and leave the umbrella at home.

Average High/Low Temperatures:

	J	F	M	A	M	J	J	A	S	O	N	D
High °F	47	50	55	63	73	83	90	87	80	67	53	45
°C	8	10	13	17	23	28	32	31	27	19	17	7
Low °F	33	37	42	49	59	68	75	73	65	53	41	33
°C	0	3	6	9	15	20	24	23	18	17	7	0

CLOTHING

Requirements for dressing in Las Vegas have fluctuated over the years, from the formality of the 1940s through the 1960s to the T-shirts and shorts of the 1980s and 1990s. Today's styles range from upscale casual to downright shoddy, with everything imaginable in between. Little is out of place here, though remember that some nicer restaurants require jackets for the men.

Remember also to pack clothing appropriate for the weather; short sleeves and skirts or shorts are accepted and nearly required for spending time outside in the summer months. Heavy winter jackets are what most winter visitors forget to pack, not expecting the chill of the winds that frequently assail the city. Sunblock is a must; a style-appropriate hat, or at least a pair of sunglasses, is highly recommended.

COMPLAINTS

Usually complaints are handled quickly and on the spot by well-intended casino managers. Always ask to speak with one if the person with whom you are dealing cannot solve the problem. If this does not help, call the **Better Business Bureau**, Tel. (702) 320-4500, or the **Consumer Affairs Division**, Tel. (702) 486-7355.

CRIME and SAFETY

Las Vegas is a fairly safe place considering the high volume of tourist traffic with which it must contend. Hotel security is notoriously efficient (look up; the black glass bubbles on the ceiling are a marker of security cameras monitored 24 hours a day), and Metro police bicycle patrols help curb problems along the Strip and Downtown. Still, standard big city precautions should be taken. Avoid dark areas, especially Downtown. Pick-pocketing on city buses and in crowded areas—such as the Treasure Island pirate show or Mirage volcano display—is notorious, so watch your suitcases, purse, or wallet. In any emergency, dial 911 from any phone; no coins needed.

But visitors are much more likely to become a victim of an accident than they are a crime. Las Vegas tourists walking down the Strip often become distracted by all the visual stimuli, so much so that between 1995 and 1997 134 pedestrians were killed by motorists. In many cases, the pedestrians were at fault, meandering into streets while looking at the lights, foolishly crossing the Strip's eight lanes of bumper-to-bumper traffic between lights, or simply backing into a lane of traffic while angling for a photograph. When walking in Las Vegas it is crucial to remember that, despite the temptation, one should not jaywalk or hop over barricades meant to prohibit pedestrian travel. Motorists are notoriously possessive of their travel lanes, and laws are set against pedestrians that violate the travel lane beyond a crosswalk.

CUSTOMS and ENTRY FORMALITIES

Citizens of Canada and Mexico do not need visas or passports, but must show proof of residency. Citizens of all the western European nations (except Greece, Portugal, and Vatican City), as well as Australia, New Zealand, and Japan can stay for up to 90 days without a visa, so long as they have a valid passport and return ticket. All others entering the US need visas.

Adult visitors staying longer than 72 hours may bring along the following items duty free: 1 liter of wine or liquor; 100 cigars (non-Cuban), or 3 pounds of tobacco, or 200 cigarettes (though they are so cheap here, one wonders why); and gifts valued under $100. Absolutely no food (including canned goods) or plants of any type are permissible.

Visitors may also arrive and depart with up to $10,000 currency without declaration.

D

DRIVING

Driving is a necessity for anyone who wishes to get around the city beyond the tourist areas, but it can be a harrowing experience. Suffering the combined factors of distracted tourists and a growing resident population from all across the world, Las Vegas streets are busy and the drivers aggressive and unpredictable. Roads that are complete are in very good condition, owing to their recent widening and paving. But there are many roadways under perpetual expansion and construction, making every day a new, frustrating experience.

Drive on the right side of the street. Right turns on red lights are permitted unless posted, as are U-turns. When a signal turns green, carefully check both directions before proceeding; Las Vegans are notorious for their attempts (and failures) to beat the traffic signal.

Watch for school crossing zones; fines are high and patrols common. Do not drink and drive; penalties are stiff and include immediate jailing.

Freeways are the I-15 traveling north from Los Angeles to Salt Lake City, and US 93/95, which comes from Arizona towards Utah.

Parking is incredibly easy, with every hotel offering free parking lots or structures (Downtown requires a casino cage validation). Valet parking is a free at-the-door service, but tips are customary. Remember that on busy nights, the valet may take longer to retrieve your car than you could have if you parked yourself (see TIPPING).

Gasoline is plentiful, available on nearly every corner and, though expensive by US standards, very inexpensive compared to elsewhere in the world, especially Europe.

E

ELECTRIC CURRENT

All of the United States uses a 110-120 volt 50-cycle alternating current (AC). Adapters are required for appliances using European or any non-standard voltage, and widely available.

EMBASSIES, CONSULATES, and HIGH COMMISSIONS

All embassies are located in the US capital, Washington, DC. Many countries also have consulates in Los Angeles or San Francisco. Locally, only Ecuador, Germany, and Italy have consulate offices. For additional embassy or consulate information, you will need to call Washington, DC. Some numbers are listed below; for others, phone Washington, DC directory assistance at (202) 555-1212.

Australia	(202) 797-3000
Canada	(202) 682-1740
Republic of Ireland	(202) 462-3939
New Zealand	(202) 328-4848
United Kingdom	(202) 462-1340
South Africa	(202) 232-4400

EMERGENCIES

Dial **911** from any phone, toll-free.

G

GAY and LESBIAN TRAVELERS

While Las Vegas may have a reputation as Sin City, it is only quietly tolerant of its fairly large gay and lesbian community, in the same look-the-other-way manner in which many gay entertainers have been accepted, but not discussed. Many gay businesses, bars, and nightclubs are centered in the small but energetic Gay Triangle, an area off Paradise Road between Harmon and Tropicana. For detailed information, pick up either of the free newspapers, *Las Vegas Bugle* or *Q-Tribe*, available in the Triangle businesses or city-wide at all major record and bookstores (Tower, Borders, Bookstar, Barnes & Noble).

GETTING THERE (see also AIRPORT and DRIVING)

There are only three modern methods of transport available for passengers coming to Las Vegas: air, bus, or automobile, though there are plans to begin casino-sponsored train service from Los Angeles, which would arrive at the Downtown train station.

By Air

Las Vegas, though a major travel destination, is still considered a second-tier city when it comes to direct flights. While most major US cities, especially in the west, offer direct flights into McCarran International (the city's only major airport), many east coast cities use hubs such as Denver, Chicago, and Phoenix. While some airlines add new direct flights on occasion, others withdraw theirs.

On an international level, direct flights come in from Tokyo (twice weekly), Frankfurt, and London (once each, weekly), though the London flight is on a scheduled charter. Call the **Convention and Visitors Authority** at (702) 892-0711 for information about international direct flights; call your airline regarding other flights.

By Bus

Greyhound Bus Lines offers daily bus travel to and from Las Vegas and surrounding cities. Call 1-800-231-2222 (toll-free in the US) for information.

GUIDES and TOURS

Numerous tour operators are located in Las Vegas, and their advertisements can be seen in every free tourist guide available along the Strip and in hotel rooms. The majority of them specialize in tours of Southern Nevada's lake, mountains, Hoover Dam and Boulder City, as well as bus and plane day-trips to the Grand Canyon (see page 68).

Only a few companies specialize in tours of the city, taking busloads of sightseers past elaborate homes (or former homes) of stars, as well as attractions like the Ethel M. Chocolate Factory and the Fremont Street Experience. **Las Vegas Tour Center**, Tel. (702) 384-1234, offers several of these city tours, including a nearly nine-hour ride for under $30.

H

HEALTH and MEDICAL CARE

Las Vegas is a modern city with modern health care and food standards. In the event of emergency, there are seven area hospitals that provide 24-hour emergency care. Travelers needing medical attention in a non-emergency situation should seek out a **University Medical Center Quick Care** clinic, with seven citywide locations. They require no appointments, and accept any patient, but be prepared to wait up to an hour or two. If you have no health insurance (or insurance not recognized), be prepared to pay for services immediately.

Complementing this, there are several 24-hour pharmacies for prescription and non-prescription drugs. Both **Walgreen's** (Las Vegas Boulevard at Charleston Boulevard) and **White Cross Drugs** (further north) are open 24 hours.

Las Vegas

HOLIDAYS

Holidays will not affect most travelers in the manner of closing. Hotel-casinos and resorts never close regardless of the day or time. Grocery stores keep shorter hours on Christmas and Thanksgiving (last Thursday of November). Government offices, schools, the post office, and banks are closed for 11 national holidays. Holidays will affect travelers during busy airport days. The Thanksgiving holiday is the busiest travel day in Las Vegas, with Christmas also being very busy.

L

LANGUAGE

English is the language of the United States, but most major hotels offer on-site interpreters of Spanish, French, German, and many Asian languages.

LAUNDRY and DRY CLEANING

Most hotel-casinos offer dry cleaning and laundry service. Outside of the hotels, the reputable chain **Al Phillips the Cleaner** offers 14 citywide locations with drive-through service and one day return.

M

MEDIA

Unlike most American cities, Las Vegas is home to two daily **news-papers**: the morning *Review-Journal* and the afternoon *Sun*. The *R-J* has a more national orientation, while the *Sun* feels like the locally-owned metropolitan daily that it is. Hotel newsstands carry both, as well as the *New York Times, Los Angeles Times, USA Today,* and *Wall Street Journal*. For a wider selection of international newspapers, try Borders Bookshop, with two locations.

There are a dozen **free local tourist guides**, ranging from small booklets of ads to more elaborate magazines with informational content and listings. The two best are *What's On* and *Showbiz Weekly*. *What's On* is available in most hotel lobbies and on news racks, while *Showbiz* is found in hotel rooms throughout the city.

Las Vegas also has two **free alternative newsweeklies**, *CityLife* and the *Las Vegas Weekly*. They are available citywide in coffeehouses, cafes, bookstores, clubs, bars, and newspaper racks, and contain extensive listings of off-Strip information.

The valley's **television** is primarily served by Cox Communications cable system, with over 60 channels. Most hotel rooms usually have at least these stations: CNN, MTV, and USA networks, plus local affiliates ABC (channel 13), CBS (channel 8), FOX (channel 5), NBC (channel 3), and PBS (channel 10).

Radio listeners are also well served in the city, with a full dial on both AM and FM bands. The primary stations are KNPR (89.5FM, classical and NPR news), KUNV (91.5FM, jazz), KOMP (92.3FM, rock), KWNR (95.5FM, country-western), KXPT (97.1FM, classic and soft rock); KXTE (107.5FM, alternative rock), KDWN (720AM, talk), and KNEWS (970AM, news).

MONEY MATTERS

Currency. The monetary unit in the US, the dollar, is based on the decimal system, with 100 pennies per dollar. The United States is in the midst of converting its well-known paper currency to a bold new design, but compared to the old, it appears almost fake. If you aren't sure, ask a casino cage. Common banknotes are in the $1, $5, $10, $20, $50, and $100 denominations. There are also dollar coins.

Currency exchange. While banks and other financial offices will exchange currency, there is no need; major casino cages will do so immediately and without commissions. This should be the traveler's first choice for exchanging cash.

Credit cards. It is strongly advised that you have at least one credit card with you while in Las Vegas. With the advent of checking-based VISA cards, their acceptance is nearly universal for almost any purchase. You will still, however, need some cash for tipping (see TIPPING).

Travelers' checks. Travelers' checks are accepted almost everywhere, though their relative hassle compared to credit cards makes them best for transporting cash between home and the casino cage, which will convert them into American currency as you require.

Las Vegas

ATMs are extraordinarily accessible throughout all major casinos. Beware of additional service fees—often up to $2—which are listed on the ATM.

Taxes. Taxation in Nevada is generally low in comparison to other US cities, thanks to heavy taxes on gaming revenue. Sales tax on merchandise and restaurant food is 7.25%; food (groceries) purchased in stores is exempt from sales tax. Lodging taxes are 7 percent, except Downtown, where they are 9 percent.

ON-LINE RESOURCES

If you want to investigate Las Vegas on-line before you leave home, here are some places to do it:

<www.vegas.com> Operated by the parent company of the *Las Vegas Sun, Showbiz Weekly, Las Vegas Life,* and *Las Vegas Weekly,* this is perhaps the most comprehensive collection of original news and information about the city on the Net.

<www.lasvegas.com> Hosted by the competitors of vegas.com, this fairly comprehensive site features news from the *Las Vegas Review-Journal,* plus community partner links to numerous important local agencies and institutions; especially helpful for relocation.

<www.well.com/user/nitewalk/guide> Maintained by a local webmaster and former journalist, this site has an original guide to local alternative culture as well as links to most of the best cultural web sites and those with other—more edgy—Las Vegas material. Definitely the on-line source for the flip side of Vegas life.

OPENING HOURS

Las Vegas is a 24-hour town. The hotel-casinos and all bars never close. Though all casinos have at least one 24-hour coffee shop, surprisingly, most restaurants keep shorter hours, closing by 10pm, 11pm on Saturday and Sunday. Retail shops and malls, both on- and off-Strip, open between 9 and 10am, closing at about 9pm (the Forum Shops are open until midnight). Grocery and many drugstores are open 24 hours.

P

PHOTOGRAPHY and VIDEO

Most hotel-casinos prohibit photography or videotaping inside the gaming areas. Check with the front desk or security desk if you aren't sure. Violating this rule could result in the confiscation of your film.

Before dropping off your film at a convenient Strip-located photo developer, remember that the proximity of the service results in what is sometimes a hefty surcharge. Call around the city for a comparison, and ask for a total estimate before using any service.

POLICE (see also CRIME AND SAFETY)

With 1.3 million residents and 30 million visitors annually, Las Vegas police take their work very seriously. They are generally helpful and friendly, and will guide tourists in the right direction if asked. Casually uniformed bicycle patrols on the Strip and in Downtown have helped the situation, with those particular officers more inclined to help with a smile and a handshake. Call 911 if you have an emergency which requires their assistance.

POST OFFICES

Local post offices are open 8am–5pm on weekdays and 9am–1pm on Saturdays. There is a location on Industrial Road behind the Stardust Casino; use the main station on Sunset Road if you require longer operating hours (6:30am–10pm Monday–Friday; 8am–4pm Saturday).

First-class postage for a domestic 1-ounce letter is 33 cents; postcard postage is 20 cents. A letter usually takes about three days to travel cross country, less if the destination is nearer to the mailing point. For overseas mailing, a 1-ounce letter costs $1, while postcards and aerogrammes cost 50 cents each.

PUBLIC TRANSPORTATION

The only source of public transportation in Las Vegas is the **Citizens Area Transit** buses, or CAT for short. Buses along the Strip, Downtown, and the Boulder Highway run 24 hours, while the 35 or so other citywide buses run 5:30am–1:30am, seven days a week. The central station for buses is the Downtown Transportation Center, Tel. (702) 228-7433, at Stewart and Casino Center, where you can get fare and schedule information.

TAXIS

Taxis are the preferred transportation of most tourists, but be warned: they are plentiful at all hotel *porte cacheres*, but cabs are nearly impossible to obtain by the streetside hailing method. You are better off walking up to a hotel and hiring one there. Further, calling a cab from a far-flung distance often requires up to an hour-long wait (see also TIPPING).

TELEPHONE

The country code for the US is 1; the area code for all of Clark County (where Las Vegas is located) is 702. While in the Las Vegas area, local calls to the metropolitan vicinity (including Henderson, Boulder City, and Mt. Charleston) require only the seven-digit number. Beyond the area but still in Nevada, dial 1 + 702 + (the seven-digit number). Out-of-state-calls, and calls to Canada, require 1 + (area code) + (number). International calls require 011 + (country code) + (city code) + (number).

TICKETS

Hotels have their own box offices for events, many of which accept over-the-phone purchases with a credit card. Tickets for some hotel events, as well as most other major events in Las Vegas (concerts, sporting events) can be purchased via **Ticketmaster** at (702) 474-4000. Remember, there are surcharges associated with using ticketing services such as Ticketmaster, so prices will be cheaper if you buy directly from the source.

TIME DIFFERENCES

The US has four time zones; Las Vegas is in the Pacific Standard Time Zone, which is eight hours behind Greenwich Mean Time. Las Vegas recognizes Daylight Savings Time; in late April, clocks move ahead one hour, and then fall back one hour in late October.

Las Vegas	New York	London	Jo'burg	Sydney
9am	12pm	5pm	7pm	3am (next day)

TIPPING

Tipping is the grease that keeps the big machine of Las Vegas operating. A majority of tourist service employees—wait staff, dealers, valets, maids, cabbies, tour guides—depend upon tips as a major portion of their income. It is suggested that you carry a selection of American currency in the $1, $5, and $10 denominations for this purpose.

Most tipping is in the $1–$3 range, but sometimes a larger tip will help things move along. No table available at a big hotel restaurant for several hours? A $10 or $20 bill will get a seat almost immediately. Valet parking full? Try $5 first, more if it is a holiday or special event. A space will magically appear. And here is a trick many overlook: if at valet pick-up a huge group of people are already waiting for their cars, waits of 20 minutes are not uncommon. A $5 bill handed to the ticket taker with a request to speed up the process will have you out quickly. When you tip under these circumstances, do so discreetly.

Restaurant tipping ranges between 15 to 20 percent of the total bill before taxes. A good tipper will go to 20 percent for extraordinary service. Be warned: Some restaurants automatically include a 12 to 15 percent surcharge for large tables; you may argue that charge if service was poor. If it is included, you may of course add a small percentage for exceptional service. Remember, if service is bad, you are not obligated to tip, but select another server the next time you visit that establishment. Here are some general suggestions:

Bartenders	$1–$2 per round for a group of two or more
Bellmen	$1 per bag
Cocktail Waitresses	$1–$2 per round
Concierges	$1 and up, depending upon their level of service
Doormen	$1 per bag, $1 for cab call
Limo Drivers	15% of total bill
Maids	$1–$2 per day, left at the end of stay
Pool Attendants	$1
Taxi Drivers	20%

Las Vegas

Valet Parking	$1–$2 when car is returned; $5–$10 to find a spot on a busy night; $5 to ticket taker for fast return
Wait Staff (Restaurant)	15–20% of total before taxes
Wait Staff (Showroom)	$5–$10

Gambling Tipping

Change Attendants	5 percent and up, depending upon your luck and their interaction
Cocktail Waitresses	$1, particularly if the drink is free; tipping with gaming chips is acceptable as well.
Dealers	If you are winning, tip the dealer by placing a bet for him or her, one-half of your bet; when leaving the table in the black, tip according to your conscience

TOURIST INFORMATION OFFICES

The **Las Vegas Convention and Visitors Authority** provides information both prior to your leaving home and after arrival. Contact them at 3150 Paradise Road, Las Vegas, NV 89109; Tel. (702) 892-0711.

W

WEIGHTS and MEASURES
The US is one of the few countries still using the SAE (Society of Automotive Engineers) standard for weights and measures instead of the metric standard.

Y

YOUTH HOSTELS

There is only one small hostel in Las Vegas, the **Las Vegas International Hostel** (Tel. 702/385-9955), located on a portion of Las Vegas Boulevard between the Strip and Downtown. The neighborhood is not the best, but safe enough during the day (travel in pairs at night) and with normal precautions. Accommodations are of the most basic sort, and available as rooms or 6-bed dorms. All bathrooms are shared, as is the kitchen. The rooms located upstairs are a bit nicer.

Recommended Hotels

By the year 2000, there were roughly 130,000 rooms in Las Vegas. This makes selecting a hotel room intimidating, but not impossible. One must consider the usual factors— cost, location, and budget—as well as how integral you want your hotel to be to your visit. It is possible, though not advisable, to visit Las Vegas and never leave your hotel premises.

The following is a recommended selection of Las Vegas's best hotels in four price categories. For a comprehensive listing of available hotels and motels, call the Las Vegas Convention and Visitors Authority (see ACCOMMODATIONS on page 109).

All businesses must comply with the Americans with Disabilities Act, and are therefore wheelchair accessible. Newer properties are the easiest to navigate, older and Downtown properties slightly more difficult.

All hotels in Las Vegas accept all major credit cards (Visa, Mastercard, American Express). Price ranges listed do not include suites. Expect holiday and weekend rates to be significantly higher, and be sure to ask for specific quotes for your intended stay. For more information about most of these hotels, particularly with regard to their casinos and attractions, look in WHERE TO GO starting on page 26.

$$$$	over $200
$$$	$100–$200
$$	$50–$100
$	under $50

Along the Strip

Bally's Hotel and Casino $$$ *3645 Las Vegas Boulevard South; Tel. (702) 967-4111, toll free 1-800-644-0777; fax (702) 967-4405.* Bally's is one of the oldest hotels on the Strip, but also one of the nicest. Large rooms with a modern flair feature overstuffed furniture and subdued earth-tones. The hotel has a beautiful pool area as well. Theme: none. 2814 rooms.

Barbary Coast $$$ *3595 Las Vegas Boulevard South; Tel. (702) 737-7111, toll free 1-888-227-2279; fax (702) 894-9954.* Wedged in a corner of Las Vegas Boulevard between Bally's and the Flamingo, the rooms here offer a charming and comfortable rendition of 1900 San Francisco featuring brass beds and etched mirrors. A big draw of the hotel-casino is the recently added restaurant, Drai's. Theme: Old San Francisco. 200 rooms.

Bellagio Hotel and Casino $$$$ *3600 Las Vegas Boulevard South; Tel. (702) 693-7111, toll free 1-888-987-6667; fax (702) 693-8585.* The city's most lavish resort, Bellagio proves what kind of Italian replication $1.6 billion can buy. The standard guest rooms are satisfyingly plush, decorated in soothing shades of brown, black, and cream. Two key perks are the exceedingly comfortable beds and huge bathrooms with deep-soaking tubs and showers big enough for two. Tip: Be sure to ask for a room overlooking the dancing fountains. Theme: Italian/Mediterranean Elegance. 3005 rooms.

Caesars Palace Hotel and Casino $$$ *3570 Las Vegas Boulevard South; Tel. (702) 731-7110, toll free 1-877-427-7243; fax (702) 731-7172.* A standard-setter since its opening, elegance at Caesars seems within reach of anyone. A recent renovation—including a new tower and pool—raises the level of its already stunning accommodations. Marble and mahogany abound. Baths feature oversized marble tubs and European fixtures, and rooms are tastefully decorated with art and sculpture. Theme: Ancient Rome. 2454 rooms.

Circus-Circus Hotel and Casino $$ *2880 Las Vegas Boulevard South; Tel. (702) 734-0410, toll free 1-877-224-7287; fax*

(702) 794-3861. Circus-Circus is Las Vegas's original family-friendly, low-roller hotel-casino. The renovated lobby is classy, but one cannot expect Strip accommodations at this price without compromise. Rooms are typical chain hotel-style blue carpeting and blonde wood furniture. To stay in the newest rooms, request one in the West Tower. Theme: the Big Top, though not in the rooms. 3744 rooms.

Excalibur Hotel and Casino $$ *3850 Las Vegas Boulevard South; Tel. (702) 597-7777, toll free 1-877-750-5464; fax (702) 597-7009.* Excalibur offers a Renaissance Faire experience aimed squarely at families or travelers on a budget. Rooms are surprisingly tasteful considering the hotel's gaudy exterior, with wrought-iron accents over dark wood and contemporary touches of red, blue, and green. Theme: Medieval Fantasy. 4008 rooms.

Flamingo Hilton Las Vegas $$$ *3555 Las Vegas Boulevard South; Tel. (702) 733-3111, toll free 1-800-732-2111; fax (702) 733-3353.* The Flamingo retains its original desert oasis flavor with a large, lush tropical pool and garden area. Most rooms in the six towers have recognizably Hilton decor, with tropical accents accentuating conservative colors and rattan furniture. Theme: none. 3530 rooms.

Four Seasons Hotel Las Vegas $$$$ *3950 Las Vegas Boulevard South; Tel. (702) 730-5937 or (877) 632-5200.* The Four Seasons offers ultra-luxury accommodations on the upper floors of the Mandalay Bay tower, accessed only via a Four Seasons lobby elevator. The two-story main building houses the lobby, four restaurants and bars, health spa, and meeting rooms. A large pool set in a lush garden is available only to Four Seasons guests. Theme: none. 424 rooms.

Harrah's Las Vegas $$$ *3475 Las Vegas Boulevard South; Tel. (702) 369-5000, toll free 1-800-427-7247; fax (702) 369-*

5008. Harrah's recently underwent a $200-million renovation; the newest rooms are in the 35-story tower. Bright colors, light wood, and brass fixtures lend an upbeat feel to the accommodations. Jacuzzi tubs are available. Theme: Carnival. 2613 rooms.

Holiday Inn Boardwalk $$ *3750 Las Vegas Boulevard South; Tel. (702) 7305-2400, toll free 1-800-635-4581; fax (702) 730-3166.* Those who insist on the familiarity of a hotel chain will like the Holiday Inn on the Strip. Request a room in the recently completed tower; furnished with cherrywood and bright colors, they are preferable to the older rooms. Theme: Coney Island. 654 rooms.

Imperial Palace Hotel and Casino $$ *3535 Las Vegas Boulevard South; Tel. (702) 731-3311, toll free 1-800-634-6441; fax (702) 735-8578.* This sprawling complex houses quite a few average but comfortable rooms. The adventurous can rent a suite with a mirrored Jacuzzi tub and mirrored ceiling over the bed. The pool area with waterfall is large and beautiful. Theme: Oriental Palace. 2700 rooms.

Luxor Hotel and Casino $$$ *3900 Las Vegas Boulevard South; Tel. (702) 262-4100, toll free 1-800-288-1000; fax (702) 262-4452.* The Luxor consists of a 30-story Egyptian pyramid and two adjacent towers. The Egyptian-themed rooms in the pyramid have one sloping glass wall overlooking the main floor, and most have a shower but no tub (rooms in the tower, however, do have tubs). The uniquely designed rooms feature Art Deco and Egyptian-inspired furnishings, with marble bathrooms. Many family-friendly attractions are on-site. Theme: Ancient Egypt. 4400 rooms.

Mandalay Bay Resort and Casino $$$ *3950 Las Vegas Boulevard South; Tel. (702) 632-7000 or (877) 632-7800.* Guests at the Mandalay will enjoy an 11-acre tropical environment, including a wave pool, a House of Blues, an enormous spa, and a number of trendy new restaurants. Theme: Tropical Jungle City. 3300 rooms.

MGM Grand Hotel and Casino $$$ *3799 Las Vegas Boulevard South; Tel. (702) 891-7777, toll free 1-877-880-0880; fax (702) 891-1030.* Four distinct towers result in four distinct room themes. The nicest are in the Hollywood tower, with gold-speckled walls surrounding maple and cherry furniture. Gilded accents and framed photos of classic film stars add up to a classy experience. The other towers—Casablanca, Old South, and Oz—have rooms distinct to their names as well. Theme: City of Entertainment. 5034 rooms.

Mirage Hotel and Casino $$$ *3400 Las Vegas Boulevard South; Tel. (702) 791-7111, toll free 1-800-374-9000; fax (702) 791-7446.* A beautiful Polynesian resort, despite being the oldest of the city's new additions. The rooms have a distinctive beach resort feel, with subdued neutral colors and gold accents. Most have marbled entries and baths, as well as canopied beds. Though the rooms are somewhat small, they are among the nicest on the Strip. Theme: South Seas. 3000 rooms.

Monte Carlo Hotel and Casino $$$ *3770 Las Vegas Boulevard South; Tel. (702) 730-7777, toll free 1-888-529-4828; fax (702) 730-7250.* Striking in its beautifully understated European theme, this resort captures an air of popular elegance. The outdoor area is lush, boasting a wave pool, waterfalls, and a river. Rooms are classically European in flavor and very comfortable. Theme: Old European Elegance. 3200 rooms.

New York-New York Hotel and Casino $$$ *3790 Las Vegas Boulevard South; Tel. (702) 740-6969, toll free 1-888-696-9887; fax (702) 740-6700.* Taking theming to its extreme, rooms here are done in 62 unique styles, all related to the "Big

Apple." Art Deco is the overall inspiration, with round-top furnishings and inlaid wood galore. On average, the rooms (and their bathrooms) are small, but the overall experience is nice. Theme: New York City. 2034 rooms.

Paris Hotel and Casino $$$ *3655 Las Vegas Boulevard South; Tel. (702) 946-7000, toll free 1-877-796-2096; fax (702) 946-4405.* The Paris Hilton triples its presence with this resort, modeled after the French Hôtel de Ville. It includes numerous replicas of Parisian landmarks, including the Eiffel Tower, Rue de la Paix, the Paris Opera House, the Louvre, and the Arc de Triomphe. Expect it to meet all the Hilton standards you are used to. Theme: Classic France. 2916 rooms.

Riviera Hotel and Casino $$ *2901 Las Vegas Boulevard South; Tel. (702) 734-5110, toll free 1-800-634-6753; fax (702) 794-9451.* One of the older Strip resorts, the Monaco and Monte Carlo towers house the newest, nicest rooms, each richly decorated with mahogany furniture and burgundy fabrics. Most tower rooms offer views of the pool or mountains, while the rooms in the original 9-story structure, due to more recent construction, look only on signs, air-conditioning ducts, and the like. Theme: none. 2100 rooms.

Sahara Hotel and Casino $$ *2535 Las Vegas Boulevard South; Tel. (702) 737-2111, toll free 1-888-696-2121; fax (702) 791-2027.* A recent $100-million renovation went the standard route, replacing a dark and plush atmosphere with lighter decor. The result has been one of attractive comfort for tour groups, conventioneers, and mid-budget travelers. Rooms are bright, with standard earth-tones and wood. Theme: Moroccan Palace. 1758 rooms.

Stardust Resort and Casino $$ *3000 Las Vegas Boulevard South; Tel. (702) 732-6111, toll free 1-800-824-6033; fax (702) 732-6257.* Think of the Stardust as an adult-oriented gambling playground. The newest guest rooms are in the two towers: the west tower decor consists of earth-tones with black accents, while the east tower rooms have lighter colors and floral prints. Guest rooms are comfortable, though not very exciting. Theme: none. 2500 rooms.

Stratosphere Hotel and Casino $$ *2000 Las Vegas Boulevard South; Tel. (702) 380-7777, toll free 1-800-998-6937; fax (702) 383-5334.* No, there are no rooms in the big tower, unfortunately. They are instead in one of the mid-rise towers, and are very comfortable, nicely decorated with Art Deco touches and black lacquer. The Las Vegas Boulevard location—not quite Strip, not quite Downtown—leaves the Stratosphere out on its own. Theme: none. 1444 rooms.

Treasure Island at the Mirage $$$ *3300 Las Vegas Boulevard South; Tel. (702) 894-7111, toll free 1-800-288-7206; fax (702) 894-7446.* Affordably elegant and comfortable—though not elaborate—rooms are housed in a Y-shaped tower. The Caribbean theme is pervasive, and the colors are similar to the casino: parchment and washed yellows. Rooms facing the Strip view the Pirate Battle, though you may not see much. Other rooms view the Mirage or the mountains. Theme: Pirates of the Caribbean. 2900 rooms.

Tropicana Resort and Casino $$$ *3801 Las Vegas Boulevard South; Tel. (702) 739-2222, toll free 1-888-826-8767; fax (702) 739-5425.* Aimed at adult travelers, the hotel is a slice of subtly-themed Polynesia—bamboo and wood dominate the environment. Guest rooms in the Island tower have a tropical theme, while the Paradise tower's rooms lean toward French Provincial. The tropical pool area (with swim-up blackjack) is lush and relaxing. Theme: none. 2000 rooms.

The Venetian Resort Hotel-Casino **$$$** *3355 Las Vegas Boulevard South; Tel. (702) 414-1000, toll free 1-877-857-1861; fax (702) 414-1100.* Renaissance Italy is captured in dramatic architecture and landscaping including canals with operating gondolas. A four-level entertainment plaza includes a showroom, and the Grand Canal Shoppes contain 140 stores and restaurants. Theme: Traditional Venice. 3354 rooms.

Downtown

Binion's Horseshoe Hotel and Casino **$$** *128 Fremont Street; Tel. (702) 382-1600, toll free 1-800-622-6468; fax (702) 384-1574.* The Horseshoe may be the most traditional gambling joint left in town. Its flocked-wallpaper-and-velvet-drapes ambiance surrounds the highest betting limits in the world. The comfortable accommodations are modestly priced. 380 rooms.

California Hotel and Casino **$$** *12 Ogden Avenue; Tel. (702) 385-1222, toll free 1-800-634-6255; fax (702) 388-2660.* This hotel draws guests mostly from Hawaii and Asia, though all are welcome. Its decor offers a taste of the South Seas; the rooms, however, are more contemporary in style, complete with marble baths. Located off Fremont. 781 rooms.

El Cortez Hotel and Casino **$** *600 Fremont Street; Tel. (702) 385-5200, toll free 1-800-634-6703; fax (702) 385-9765.* The El Cortez (built in 1941) is the city's oldest operating casino—and unabashedly proletariat. The nicest rooms are in the 14-story tower, but the old rooms are still charming, with wood floors; all are clean and comfortable, but do not expect extravagance. 402 rooms.

Fitzgerald's Casino Hotel **$$** *301 Fremont Street; Tel. (702) 388-2400, toll free 1-800-274-5825; fax (702) 388-2478.* Many of Fitzgerald's 650 rooms offer nice views of the city and mountains within comfortable surroundings. Accommodations are of the standard Holiday Inn variety (in fact, they *are* Holiday Inn rooms) and budget-priced. Attractive views of the Fremont Street Experience can also be had in this (mostly) low-roller haven. 638 rooms.

Four Queens Hotel and Casino $$ *202 Fremont Street; Tel. (702) 385-4011, toll free 1-800-634-6045; fax (702) 387-5133.* A neon landmark since 1966, the Four Queens today entices mainly older guests. Rooms are of Southwestern or earth-tone decor and are pleasant and affordable. Four restaurants include Hugo's Cellar, an always-busy classic Las Vegas gourmet room with a winning wine list. 690 rooms.

Golden Gate Hotel and Casino $ *1 Fremont Street; Tel. (702) 385-1906, toll free 1-800-426-1906; fax (702) 382-5349.* This charming operation is the city's oldest hotel, and perhaps the only bed-and-breakfast experience in Las Vegas. Its small (10 sq ft/3 sq m) but elegant rooms, with plaster walls and mahogany doors, hearken back to another era. 106 rooms.

Golden Nugget $$$ *129 East Fremont Street; Tel. (702) 385-7111, toll free 1-800-634-3454; fax (702) 386-8362.* The 1946 Golden Nugget is the jewel of Downtown; metropolitan elegance supersedes the surrounding glitz. Guests, greeted by uniformed doormen, enter a gilded lobby full of marble and crystal. Accommodations—featuring a misted pool area landscaped with palms—are luxurious enough to have earned a top AAA rating. 1907 rooms.

Lady Luck Casino Hotel $$ *206 North Third Street; (702) 477-3000, toll free 1-800-523-9582; fax (702) 382-2346.* The rooms here—especially in the two newer towers—are very comfortable. The hotel-casino has two Downtown rarities: a showroom staging a production magic show, and a pool. 791 rooms.

Main Street Station $$ *200 North Main Street; Tel. (702) 387-1896, toll free 1-800-713-8933; fax (702) 388-2660.* Main Street Station is Las Vegas's best-kept secret. The Victorian-styled casino is filled with expensive antiques. Rooms are spacious, quiet, and simply decorated, with shutters instead of drapes. Dining options include several very good restaurants. 406 rooms.

Sam Boyd's Fremont Hotel and Casino $$ *200 East Fremont Street; Tel. (702) 385-3232, toll free 1-800-634-6460; fax (702) 385-6720.* Built in 1956 as Las Vegas's first high-rise, the Fremont's guest rooms are comfortable, modern, and decorated in a tropical-floral style. The hotel hosts many Hawaiian travelers. The Second Street Grill features Pacific Rim specialties. 452 rooms.

Off-Strip Resorts and Casinos

Alexis Park $$$ *375 East Harmon; Tel. (702) 796-3330, toll free 1-800-582-2228; fax (702) 796-4334.* A Mediterranean villa on 20 acres of beautiful landscape, this resort offers volumes beyond the typical Las Vegas hotel. Styled with classy European elegance, all rooms are suites, with ten distinct floor plans and different décor. A lack of gaming results in noticeable quiet, but the hotel is directly across from the Hard Rock Hotel if you're in the mood for gaming. 500 rooms.

Boulder Station Hotel and Casino $$ *4111 Boulder Highway, 89121; Tel. (702) 432-7777, toll free 1-800-683-7777; fax (702) 432-7744.* Located on the Boulder Strip, the Boulder Station Hotel offers a small-scale version of the inclusive upscale resort. Rooms are comfortable and attractive, but a bit higher-priced than most off-strip resorts. 300 rooms.

Gold Coast Hotel and Casino $$ *4000 West Flamingo Road; Tel. (702) 367-7111, toll free 1-888-402-6278; fax (702) 367-8575.* The Gold Coast Hotel offers a combination of entertainment and gaming, as well as a bowling center, three lounges, a dance hall, and a twin theater. Guest rooms are both comfortable and affordable. 711 rooms.

Hard Rock Hotel and Casino $$$ *4455 Paradise Road; Tel. (702) 693-5000, toll free 1-800-473-7625; fax (702) 693-5010.* A surprising exercise in casual elegance, considering its theme. Rooms are spacious and pleasing, decorated in a classic Modernist style. Light fixtures made of cymbals adorn the ceilings. All rooms have balconies, though the ones with pool views are preferable. 700 rooms.

Las Vegas Hilton Hotel and Casino $$$ *3000 South Paradise Road; Tel. (702) 732-5111, toll free 1-888-732-7117; fax (702) 732-5805.* Located next to the Convention Center, the Hilton does brisk business during large conventions. The lobby and casino are gracious and expensively outfitted, and the already plush guest rooms—each loaded with overstuffed chairs, large closets, and marble-tiled bathrooms—recently underwent a complete renovation. 3174 rooms.

Orleans Hotel and Casino $$ *4500 West Tropicana Avenue; Tel. (702) 365-7111, toll free 1-800-675-3267; fax (702) 365-7505.* The guest rooms here are among the city's largest, and an excellent bargain. They are lavishly appointed, with New Orleans-style décor in brass, antiques, and lace. 840 rooms.

Palace Station Hotel and Casino $$ *2411 West Sahara Avenue; Tel. (702) 367-2411, toll free 1-800-634-3101; fax (702) 221-6510.* Located just off the Strip near I-15, the Palace Station's newest—and best—rooms are within the tower, built in 1991, while original rooms are in a two-story building surrounding the pool. If possible, request one of the corner rooms, which have larger bathrooms. 1030 rooms.

Las Vegas

Rio Suites Hotel and Casino $$$ *3700 West Flamingo Road; Tel. (702) 252-7777, toll free 1-800-752-9746; fax (702) 252-8909.* The Rio offers such quality in mid-priced accommodations that it has received international acclaim (it's one of the city's best values). The newest rooms are in the Masquerade Tower; standard accommodations are notably the city's second largest. Guest rooms are decorated in a contemporary style of bold colors over wood. 2556 rooms.

Sam's Town Hotel and Casino $$ *5111 Boulder Highway, 89122; Tel. (702) 456-7777, toll free 1-800-634-6371; fax (702) 454-8014.* The rustic wild-West and Native American decor may sound kitschy, but the rooms here are actually quiet, comfortable, and attractive. The real treat is the nine-story atrium over an indoor park, complete with live trees, running water, and footpaths. Some in-facing rooms below the ninth floor are actually within this atrium. 650 rooms.

Showboat Hotel, Casino, and Bowling Center $$ *2800 Fremont Street, 89104; Tel. (702) 385-9123, toll free 1-800-634-3484; fax (702) 383-9238.* This remodeled New Orleans-style casino sits where Fremont Street becomes the Boulder Highway. Rooms are small but comfortable, and decorated in a Mississippi-New Orleans plantation style which is bright and uplifting. 500 rooms.

Sunset Station $$ *1301 West Sunset Road, 89119; Tel. (702) 547-7777, toll free 1-888-319-4655; fax (702) 547-7744.* The Mediterranean interior at the Sunset Station is stunning. Amenities include a 13-screen cinema and KidsQuest indoor play area, making this a sure family stop. It's located far off the Strip in Green Valley, across from a major shopping area. 450 rooms.

Recommended Restaurants

Restaurants are listed alphabetically according to location. Price ranges are per person for a typical entree at that particular location. Outstanding buffets in Las Vegas are listed in this section, with the name of the hotel first. For more information about the dining scene in Las Vegas, see EATING OUT starting on page 104.

Expect to stand in line (and pay) for a buffet before you enter. Once inside, you can eat all you wish, though it is considered unacceptable to bring food out of the buffet area. Soft drinks are often included in the price of the buffet, but beer and wine is purchased at the register. The tip is left on the table after the meal.

All of the restaurants listed below accept all major credit cards (Visa, Mastercard, and American Express).

$$$$	$30 and over
$$$	$25–$30
$$	$13–$24
$	under $12

Along the Strip

Bertolini's $$ *Caesars Palace Forum Shops; Tel. (702) 735-4663.* Lunch and dinner. This upscale franchise offers delicious Italian entrees and wood-fired pizza. Most patrons choose to dine "outdoors" near a huge (and loud) fountain.

Cheesecake Factory $$ *Caesars Palace Forum Shops; Tel. (702) 792-6888.* Breakfast, lunch, and dinner. The Factory is a cavernous restaurant with a huge menu serving an incredible variety of food. Sunday brunch (not buffet) is delicious. Though you'll be tempted to sit mall-side, don't—the statue water show is loud and disruptive.

Chinois $$$ *Caesars Palace Forum Shops; Tel. (702) 737-9700.* Lunch and dinner. Another Wolfgang Puck creation, this one an upscale Pan Asian affair. Enjoy selections from the innovative Pacific Rim menu. The café section is substantially less expensive than the dining room.

Coyote Cafe and Grill Room $$$ *MGM Grand; Tel. (702) 891-7349.* Breakfast, lunch, and dinner. Mark Miller's Coyote Cafe serves inspired Southwestern-nouvelle and delicious chile-filled dishes. Avoid the cafe; the good food is served in the grill.

Drai's $$$ *Barbary Coast; Tel. (702) 737-0555.* Dinner only. Restaurateur to the stars in Hollywood, Victor Drai's new eatery has made the Barbary Coast Hotel the place to eat. The menu is elaborate French nouvelle, and the appetizers are just delicious.

Emeril's $$$ *MGM Grand; Tel. (702) 891-7374.* Lunch and dinner. Seafood is almost a no-no in the desert, but Emeril Lagasse makes it a yes-yes. Imaginative preparations result in amazingly delicate seafood experiences, with a great wine list to top it off.

Mirage Buffet $ *The Mirage; Tel. (702) 791-7111.* Breakfast, lunch, and dinner. Another excellent, all-you-can-eat feast. Though a little expensive, the overall quality, fabulous salad selection, and delicious desserts make this a winner.

Noodles $$ *Bellagio; Tel. (702) 693-8131.* Lunch and dinner. A modern Tony Chi-designed Pan Asian noodle shop in the heart of Las Vegas. The Modernist touches are elegantly trendy, and the variety of menu selections vast and very authentic.

Palm $$$$ *Caesars Palace Forum Shops; Tel. (702) 732-7256.* Lunch and dinner. A steakhouse of near perfection that also happens to serve lobster. The wine list is very extensive, including by-the-glass choices. Avoid sitting "outside," as the noise level is very high.

Spago $$$ *Caesars Palace Forum Shops; Tel. (702) 369-6300.* Lunch and dinner. One of the first Los Angeles eateries to introduce fusion cooking techniques, Wolfgang Puck's famous restaurant is as much about being seen there as it is eating there. A French-, Asian-, and Italian-inspired menu ends with fabulous desserts.

Top of the World $$$$ *Stratosphere Tower; Tel. (702) 380-7777.* Lunch and dinner. The food often takes second place here, as the revolving restaurant offers diners a full-circle view of Las Vegas every hour. Though the view is unparalleled, the continental cuisine is done well, too.

Tre Visi $$ *MGM Grand; Tel. (702) 891-7220.* Breakfast, lunch, and dinner. An informal café attached to a more formal dining room, this pair turns the tables on your expectations. The café is the more desirable of the two, featuring delicious Tuscan specialties and light and flavorful pizzas.

Downtown

Bay City Diner $ *Golden Gate Hotel; Tel. (702) 382-3510.* Open 24 hours a day. The Bay City Diner is a 24-hour café with a twist. A dark wood interior and turn-of-the-century feel lend a pleasant ambiance to accompany the standard coffee shop menu.

Binion's Ranch Steakhouse $$$ *Binion's Horseshoe; Tel. (702) 382-1600.* Dinner only. Some of the best beef in the west comes through this steakhouse (the Binions are ranchers as well as casino-owners). The 24th-floor view of the city is nice, too.

Garden Court Buffet $ *Main Street Station; Tel. (702) 387-1896.* A beautiful, relaxing buffet experience set under high ceilings, surrounded by marble and brick. Multiple food stations allow one to sample everything from wood-fired pizza to Mexican and Asian specialties.

Hugo's Cellar $$$ *Four Queens; Tel. (702) 385-4011.* Dinner only. An excellent wine list complements this unexpected Downtown gem. The continental cuisine is a bit dated, but the experience is elegant and romantic.

The Buffet $ *Golden Nugget Hotel; Tel. (702) 385-7111.* Breakfast, lunch, and dinner. This is the buffet that set the modern standard. An elegant and comfortable dining room accommodates diners who select from a huge variety of well-executed, all-you-can-eat fare.

Triple 7 Brewpub $ *Main Street Station; Tel. (702) 387-1896.* Open 11am–7am. The Triple 7 Brewpub is a virtually unknown (in Las Vegas) delight. Ales and beers brewed on the premises complement a fresh and innovative menu of American and Asian cuisine, as well as delicious wood-fired pizzas.

Off-Strip

Benihana Village $$ *Las Vegas Hilton (702) 732-5821.* Dinner only. The same Benihana you may have been to before: a Japanese-themed eatery set in an elaborate garden. Energetic chefs entertain large tables of strangers by cooking Japanese food in front of them.

Carnival World Buffet $ *Rio Suites Hotel and Casino; Tel. (702) 252-7757.* Breakfast, lunch, and dinner. The main attractions here are the numerous cooked-to-order food stations ranging from Asian to Mexican to Italian. The buffet combines a fresh-food approach with the mass-audience aesthetic.

Chicago Joe's $–$$ *820 South Fourth Street; Tel. (702) 382-5637.* Lunch and dinner. A tiny restaurant in a former Downtown home, Joe's has been serving tasty southern Italian pastas and shellfish for over 20 years.

Dona Maria's $ *910 Las Vegas Boulevard South; Tel. (702) 382-6538.* Lunch and dinner. Dona Maria's is an authentic Mexican restaurant, specializing in tamales. Try the hot pork, mild chicken, and chile-and-cheese varieties.

The Feast Buffet $ *Palace Station; Tel. (702) 367-2411.* The innovator of a modern buffet trend, The Feast is responsible for the live-action cooking now found in buffets citywide. Made-to-order omelets, multiple ethnic food stations, and a smorgasbord of desserts make this one of the best buffet bargains in town.

Golden Steer Steakhouse $$$ *308 West Sahara Avenue; Tel. (702) 384-4470.* The Golden Steer is your classic Vegas steakhouse; it has the atmosphere of a bordello. If you like big steaks served in dark booths, you'll love this place.

Hamada of Japan $$ *598 East Flamingo Road; Tel. (702) 733-3005.* A lounge, sushi bar, and dining room combine to make this a Japanese food overload. A favorite meal-time diversion is to watch your own food being cooked at the hibachi tables.

Jazzed Café and Vinoteca $ *2055 East Tropicana Avenue; Tel. (702) 798-5995.* Dinner and late-night dining. This tiny, elegant, candle-lit café serves carefully crafted Tuscan specialties— risotto, pastas, and salads—complemented by an extensive wine list. Best of all, it is open until about 4am.

Lindo Michoacan $$ *2655 East Desert Inn Road; Tel. (702) 735-6828.* Lunch and dinner. This authentic Mexican restaurant serves elaborate South-of-the-border cuisine, including roasted goat meat served with rich sauces and freshly-made flour tortillas.

Mama Marie's Cucina $$ *Rio Suites Hotel and Casino; Tel. (702) 247-7926.* Lunch and dinner. Continuing the Rio tradition, Mama Marie's serves good pasta dishes and breads at reasonable prices. You'll like the casual atmosphere as well.

Mr. Lucky's 24/7 $ *Hard Rock Hotel; Tel. (702) 693-5000.* Open 24 hours a day. Mr. Lucky's is a 24-hour hotel restaurant that breaks the mold. That is, it's nicely decorated and has a festive atmosphere. The menu offers standard American items, such as hamburgers, steak, pizza, and pasta.

Las Vegas

Mortoni's $$ *Hard Rock Hotel; Tel. (702) 693-5047.* Dinner only. Italian specialties as well as thick, juicy steaks are served in an atmosphere of sublime elegance. Ask for outdoor seating in good weather.

Papamios $$ *Sam's Town Hotel and Casino; Tel. (702) 456-7777.* Dinner only. A surprisingly elegant Italian restaurant in a library-like setting. The pastas are very good, and the entrees excellent. "Outdoor" dining is available under the atrium.

Napa Restaurant $$$$ *Rio Suites Hotel and Casino; Tel. (702) 247-7961.* Dinner only. Many Las Vegas gourmands consider Napa the finest restaurant in the state. The decidedly upscale, country-French cooking brings nouvelle cuisine to Las Vegas in force. Even the wine list is world-class.

Suzette's $$$$ *Santa Fe Hotel and Casino; Tel. (702) 658-4900.* Dinner only. Suzette's is a true French gourmet restaurant that attracts visitors all the way from the Strip. The steak tartar and lobster thermidor are particularly good here.

The Voodoo Café $$ *Rio Suites Hotel and Casino; Tel. (702) 247-7800.* Lunch and dinner. High atop the Rio, with a view overlooking all of Las Vegas, enjoy spicy Creole and Cajun specialties served in a decadent atmosphere.

Z'Tejas $$ *3824 Paradise Road; Tel. (702) 732-1660.* Lunch and dinner. Z'Tejas has elevated Southwestern cooking to an art form. You'll enjoy jalapeno chicken pasta, vegetable enchiladas, and other spicy selections served in a modern, casually elegant atmosphere.

INDEX